Spiritual Foundations
of Church Growth

Dr. Elmer Towns
Liberty University

Spiritual Foundations of Church Growth
Copyright © 2005 by Dr. Elmer Towns

Permissions Department
Academx Publishing Services, Inc.
P.O. Box 56527
Virginia Beach, VA 23456
http://www.academx.com

Printed in the United States of America

ISBN: 1-932768-09-2

Spiritual Foundations of Church Growth: Worktext

Dr. Elmer Towns

Table of Contents

CHAPTER ONE
TOWARDS SPIRITUAL GROWTH

A. ILLUSTRATIONS OF SPIRITUALITY IN THE WORK OF GOD

1. _Revival_ . My salvation/ Harrington
2. _Faith_ . Bill Bright/ 50 million
3. _Prayer_ . Maxwell/ Second Baptist Church
4. _Worship_ . Jack Hayford
5. _Fasting_ . 5 million
6. _Anointed Preaching_ . Billy Graham
7. _Intercession_ . Healings/ Charles Hughes/Vernon Brewer

B. THE CHURCH GROWS BY BOTH ORGANISM AND ORGANIZATION

ORGANISM	ORGANIZATION
Life (Internal)	Structure (External)
Feeling	Rational
Growth from inner to outer	Growth from outer to inner
Spirit-directed	Leadership
Sensitive	Management of people
Ministry	Marketing

C. SOME CHURCHES SEEM TO GROW BY ONLY AN EMPHASIS ON _Organization_ .

1. Because all _order_ in the world comes from God.
2. As a _reaction_ (echoes of past spirituality).
3. Pragmatic effect.

D. SOME CHURCHES SEEM TO GROW BY ONLY AN EMPHASIS ON _organism_ .

1. _Inner growth_ always demands _outer change_ .
2. Growing people influence where they grow.

E. BALANCE IS THE KEY TO GROWTH

1. _Internal_ growth (_Spiritual_ factors of growth in grace, the Word, conformity to Christ, attitude, etc.)
2. _External_ growth (natural factors of growth in attendance, offering, membership, baptisms, enrollment, numerical growth, etc.)
3. _Transfer_ growth.
4. _Biological_ growth.

1. cross cultural Evangelism.
2. Church planting.
3. Homogenious principle.

· Barriers to Church Growth.
· E -1 stained glass
· E - 2 class and culture barrier
· E - 3 Language Barrier

5. _Conversion_ growth.
6. Extension growth (beginning another similar type church in a similar type neighborhood).
7. Expansion growth or bridge growth (beginning another church in a different culture, i.e., cross-cultural evangelism).

F. TWO TYPES OF BALANCE

1. Balance between _spiritual_ factors and _natural_ factors.
2. Balance between leadership, organization, outreach, and discipleship.

G. THREE DEFINITIONS OF CHURCH GROWTH

1. Church Growth is _statistics_, large numbers, making lists, and statistics.
2. Church Growth is _evangelism_ by church planting, Donald McGavran.
3. Church Growth is a _behavioral science/discipline_.
   a. Gather data concerning a problem.
   b. Examine the data.
   c. Suggest a hypothesis that will solve the problem.
   d. Test the solution to verify if the principle is true.
   e. Establish a set of principles.

statistics
evangelism
behavioral science/discipline

H. FORERUNNERS OF CHURCH GROWTH

1. _John Wesley_ - new methods, i.e., Methodists. For holiness, discipline, classes, societies, etc.
2. _Southern Baptists_ - Flake's formula was early "_scientific_" principles to build Sunday school/church.
   a. Church relationships (offices and pastors).
   b. Enlargement through visitation.
   c. Grading (age-group classes).
   d. Baptist literature.
   e. Use of the Bible as text.
   f. Preaching attendance.
   g. Evangelism (attempts to lead pupils to Christ).
   h. Standards for meetings, equipment, and records.
   i. Training workers.
   j. Stewardship and mission promotion for giving.

I. LAWS OF _Sunday school Growth_

1. The law of the _teacher_ - there must be one teacher/worker for every 10 pupils.
2. The law of the _class_ - there must be one class for every 10 pupils.
3. The law of dividing and adding - new members and new units grow more rapidly than units that are older and larger.

Method is ... many, principle is few
Method is [ ] , principle never do.
is change

4. The law of ___grading___ - arrange pupils by ages for best growth.
5. The law of ___outreach___ - enrollment and attendance increase in proportion to visitation.

J. THE FULLER FACTOR

1. Donald McGavran, the ___father___ of the modern Church Growth Movement.
   a. Biblical mandate: importance of numerical growth.
   b. Focus on receptive groups.
   c. Be aware of people movements.
   d. Science is a valid tool.
   e. Right method guarantees large response. By Robertson McQuilkin.

K. ___The Ten Largest Sunday Schools___**s, 1969 PRINCIPLES DRAWN FROM THE DATABASE OF TEN CHURCHES. THEY WERE AN EARLY ATTEMPT THAT INCLUDED SPIRITUAL AND NUMERICAL FACTORS OF GROWTH.** C. Peter Wagner said this was the first book on American Church Growth and the first book on the mega church explosion that occurred at the end of the 20th Century.

L. CONTEMPORARY SETTING

1. A strong trend toward ___marketing___; i.e., Barna, *The Frog in the Kettle* and *User Friendly Churches.*
2. An opposite trend toward ___spiritual factors___; Power Evangelism
   The Third Wave
   Signs and Wonders
   Praying for the cities
   Deliverance/Binding Satan
   Discipleship

M. THE YOUNG ADULTS (BABY BOOMERS) ARE SUPERNATURALLY ORIENTED. WHERE DO THEY GET THEIR THEOLOGY?

___Movies and Music___.

N. WHO DOES GOD BLESS?

1. The doctrine of ___blessability___: i.e., those who are closest to God in faith, hope, and love (1 Cor. 13:13), and obedience to God as reflected in commitment to godliness, and service.
2. Commitment to positive, more than negative.
3. Commitment to action, more than knowledge.

THE DOCTRINE OF BLESSABILITY

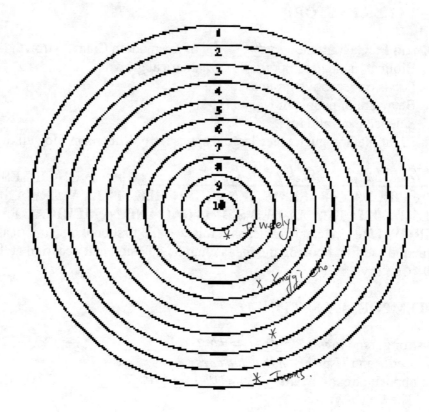

God blesses those who are closest to Him in faith,
hope, and love (I Cor. 13:13), and are most obedient
to Him as reflected in commitment to godliness and service.

CHAPTER TWO
VISIONARY LEADERSHIP: The Development of a Megachurch

A. INTRODUCTION: HISTORY OF GROWING CHURCHES

"When Elmer Towns published his book [*The Ten Largest Sunday Schools*, 1969], only ninety-seven churches across the United States were known to have one thousand or more in attendance. Three decades later, there are six to eight thousand such churches." (Elmer Towns and Warren Bird, *Into the Future*, page 177)

1. Great churches during the post-apostolic church
   a. Great _buildings_
   b. Leadership _training centers_, i.e. leaders and students
   c. Energetic center of influence
   d. Source for the spread of the Gospel

2. Dark Ages
   a. _Monasteries_
   b. Built and led by great pioneering founders
   c. Influence and outreach

3. Reformers
   a. Martin Luther
   b. John Calvin, i.e., Geneva
   c. John Wesley, i.e., traveled, built churches, built followers, new methods, i.e., Methodist

---

Core Values in Growing Churches
(*Into the Future*, page 188)

1. Evangelism theology . . . of _aggressive outreach_
2. Strong _pastoral leadership_
3. _participatory_ worship
4. Powerful _prayer_
5. Centrality of the _Holy Spirit_
6. Abundant finances . . . _through tithing_
7. _Lay ministry_
8. _Practical_ Bible teaching
9. _Direct_ missions involvement
10. _Low denominational profile_

B. GREAT CHURCHES IN AMERICA

1. Center from Boston to Philadelphia to Wheaton. Where is next center?

2. Two forces that produce great churches, i.e., _the interstate_
    (transportation) and _the Internet_ (communication).

3. A new methodology, i.e. Church Growth _as a science_.
    a. State a problem
    b. Gather data
    c. Suggest a hypothesis to answer the problem
    d. Test the suggested hypothesis
    e. Establish a new principle/law

4. *The Ten Largest Sunday Schools* (Baker Book House, 1969)
    A data pool of ten churches from which conclusive information could be drawn.
    These were predictive of the future. According to C. Peter Wagner, this was the
    first _American church Growth_ book, and the first book
    on the _megachurch_.

    a. "Great men build great churches." – Beauchamp Vick
    b. Focus: "Preach the Gospel and put walls around it." – H. Henninger
    c. "To build a great church, do three things: First, _advertise_ to
        get people there. Second, _evangelize_ to get them saved.
        Third, _raise money_ to pay for the endeavor." – B. Vick
    d. Busing – "_An anointed method_."
    e. What is an anointed method? Can methods be anointed?
    f. There were three great streams that flowed into a river that originally built
        these churches:
        (1) _Pietism_ - Holiness/Knowing God
        (2) _Revivalism_ - God pours Himself on His people.
        (3) _Evangelism_ - Soul-winning
    g. Fundamental Christianity
        (1) A return to the _essentials_
        (2) More than a theological movement, it is a _social movement_.
        (3) What is fundamentalism?
            a) Inerrancy of Scriptures,
            b) Virgin birth (deity),
            c) Vicarious substitutionary atonement,
            d) Bodily resurrection,
            e) Physical return of Christ.
    h. History of the Hot One, i.e., anointed method
        50s   Lee Roberson   _House – to – house visitation_
        60s   Jack Hyles   _Buses_
        70s   Jerry Falwell   _Saturation evangelism /media_

> ## Saturation Evangelism
> "Using every available means to reach every available person at every available time."

80s	John MacArthur	*Preaching evangelism*
90s	Bill Hybels	*Seeker – driven church*
2000	Jack Hayford	*Praise and worship church*

> ## Praise and Worship Methodology
> "If you worship Him, He will come."

| 2010 | David Yonggi Cho | *Small cell groups* |

> ## Cell Groups Methodology
> "The body grows by the division of cells."

5. Explosion of mega churches (large, mega, super, stretch-cell, multiple-congregational, extended geographical parish church)
   a. Explosive research of 70s and 80s produced large churches

Models	-	Pre
Paradigms	-	Process
Case Studies	-	Post

   b. Paradigms of growing churches (glue)

Hybels	*Evangelistic*	– intentional outreach
MacArthur	*Bible expositional*	- teaching
Hayford	*Renewal*	– to touch God and be touched by God
Cho	*Body life*	– Koinonia fellowship
D. James Kennedy	*Liturgical*	– worship
Maxwell/Garlow	*Congregational*	– member driven

   c. The interstate and the ___*Internet*___
   d. Awareness of ___*Spiritual giftedness*___ in each model
      1) Gift ___*Imposing*___
      2) Gift ___*Gravitation*___
      3) Gift ___*Assimilation*___
      4) Gift ___*Manipulation*___

6. Great churches focused on growing leadership
   1. Allowance for leadership
   2. Awareness of the need of leadership
   3. Developing leadership
   4. Tension between leadership and tradition

C. METHODOLGY OF MEGACHURCHES

According to Lyle Schaller, "The emergence of the 'megachurch' is the most important development of modern Christian history." (Elmer Towns and Warren Bird, *Into the Future*, page 179)

> "Healthy churches do not pay staff to do ministry. They equip the laity to do ministry." – Bill Easum

Grow Bigger by Learning to "Do Small Well" (Elmer Towns and Warren Bird, *Into the Future*, pages 183,184)

1. The key for success in the large church is a well-coached _System of small groups_ focused on quality of care.
2. "The church must grow _larger and smaller_ at the same time." – Rick Warren
3. "The church of the future will not be a church _with small groups_, but it will be a church _of small groups_ where membership in a small group will be more primary than church membership." – George Hunter

---

Potential Strengths of Larger Churches
(*Into the Future*, page 183)

1. Large churches develop when a church reaches out to more and more people who are put in a _right relationship with God_.
2. The large church is able to evangelize an _entire metropolism area_.
3. The large church provides all the _spiritual gifts_ to the local church.
4. The large church can be a _conscience_ to the community and can speak out on social issues in a community.
5. The large church can be _self-supporting_.

CHAPTER THREE
THE LAWS OF LEADERSHIP

You are controlled by _____ **of your position.**

A. THE EIGHT LAWS OF LEADERSHIP
(From *The Eight Laws of Leadership* by Elmer Towns, Church Growth Institute, Lynchburg, VA, 1992)

1. Law One: The Law of Vision/Dreams
   a. Descriptive statement: People follow a leader who directs them to a desirable objective.
   b. Prescriptive statement: Leaders must direct followers to a desirable objective.
   c. *Slogan:* _____

   _____.
   d. Keep in mind:
      1) "Vision is seeing opportunities through _____."
      2) You can't manage or organize a church into greatness, but you can't have a great church _____ management and organization.
      3) Vision takes different forms for different people.

2. Law Two: The Law of Rewards.
   a. Descriptive statement: People follow a leader who provides them rewards from their self-chosen goals.
   b. Prescriptive statement: Leaders must reward those who follow them.
   c. *Slogan:* _____.
   d. Types of rewards
      1) Ego
      2) Monetary
      3) Appreciation
      4) Achievement
      5) Promotion
      6) Money

3. Law Three: The Law of Credibility.
   a. Descriptive statement: People follow a leader when they have confidence in his plans.
   b. Prescriptive statement: Leaders must have a credibility plan to reach the objective.
   c. *Slogan:* _____

   _____.

d. How to gain credibility:
1) You believe in them first, then they believe in you.
2) Character is who you are when no one in watching.
3) "Carefully avoid in yourself those things which disturb you in others" – Thomas À Kempis
4) "Property may be destroyed and money may lose its purchasing power; but character, health, knowledge and good judgment will always be in demand under all conditions." – Roger Babson
5) What lies behind us and what lies before us are tiny matters compared to what lies within us." – Ralph Waldo Emerson

4. Law Four: The Law of Communication.
a. Descriptive statement: People follow a leader who effectively communicates his plan to reach the objective.
b. Prescriptive statement: Leaders must effectively communicate their plans to reach the objective.
c. *Slogan:* _____
_____.
d. Keep in mind:
1) Preaching is what _____; communicating is what _____.

5. Law Five: The Law of Accountability.
a. Descriptive statement: People follow a leader who gives them responsibility to help reach the objective.
b. Prescriptive statement: Leaders must know the contribution that their followers make to help reach the goal.
c. *Slogan:* _____
_____.

6. Law Six: The Law of Motivation.
a. Descriptive statement: People follow a leader who gives them compelling reasons to reach the objective.
b. Prescriptive statement: Leaders must motivate followers to accomplish the objective.
c. *Slogan:* _____
_____.

7. Law Seven: The Law of Problem-Solving.
a. Descriptive statement: People follow a leader who gives solutions to problems that hinder them from reaching the objective.
b. Prescriptive statement: Leaders must solve problems that hinder followers from reaching their objective.
c. *Slogan:* _____
_____.

8. Law Eight: The Law of Decision-Making.
   a. Descriptive statement: People follow a leader who gives answers to the decisions involving their objective.
   b. Prescriptive statement: Leaders must make good decisions that move followers toward the objective.
   c. *Slogan*: _____
   _____
   _____.

   d. Becoming a good decision maker:
      1) Information acquiring: good pastors must know how to get information about his church
      2) Information processing is important – ask yourself, "What is important and what isn't?"
      3) Information storing – there are certain things you must never forget and you must know where to find them and how to use them.

B. DEVELOPING LAY LEADERSHIP
(From *Into the Future*, Elmer Towns and Warren Bird, Fleming H. Revell, 2000, pages 163-174)

God's purpose for pastors (as well as teachers, evangelists, prophets, and apostles) is to "prepare God's people for works of service, so that the body of Christ may be built up until we all reach unity in the faith and in the knowledge of the Son of God and become mature, attaining to the whole measure of the fullness of Christ." – Eph. 4:12-13

> "The pastoral team, the staff of the church, is to serve the people of the church in *their* ministry – to empower *them*, to equip *them*, to give *them* tracks to run on for ministry." – Ted Haggard.
>
> "Today, the pastor needs to come to the laypeople and say, 'How can I help *your* ministry?'" – Loren Mead

1. Build Churches through _____:
2. According to Bill Easum, "Churches grow when they intentionally reach out to people instead of concentrating on their _____. Churches die when they concentrate on _____."
   a. Forces behind lay ministry expansions
      1) The assumption that laypeople can be trusted.
      2) High expectations on membership within the church.
      3) Recognition that it is a progression within a believer's life from seeker to believer to learner to disciple.
      4) The professional nature of a large segment of the population.
      5) A compelling recognition that ministry is satisfying and rewarding.
   b. Growth is not concerned with numbers, but with _____
   _____.

   c. According to George Barna, "Groups and teams of _____ _____, effectively networked together, are fundamental to virtually every healthy church in the world."

   d. "Megachurches survive only because they encourage attenders to bond in _____." – Lyle Schaller

2. Build lay leadership on _____ .

   a. There is effectiveness when all members minister in the church according to their strengths and desires, "We have different gifts, according to the grace given to us." – Romans 12:16

   b. Elements of a team-based church

      1) A covenant team
      2) A visionary team
      3) A culture-creating team
      4) A collaborative team
      5) A trusting team
      6) An empowering team
      7) A learning team.

Leaders who Develop Followers	Leaders who Develop Leaders
Need to be _____	Want to be _____
Focus on _____	Focus on _____
Develop the _____ 20 percent	Develop the _____ 20 percent
Treat their people the same for "fairness"	Treat their leaders as individuals for impact
_____ power	
_____ time with others	_____ time in others
Grow by _____	Grow by _____
Impact only people they touch personally.	Impact people far beyond their own reach

(From John Maxwell, *21 Irrefutable Laws of Leadership*, page 133)

APPLICATION QUESTIONS

1. Which "Law of Leadership" gave you an "Aha!" insight? Why?

2. In which "Law of Leadership" are you strongest? Why? How can you capitalize further on that strength?

3. What principle from this message do you need to apply most vigorously as you go home? Why?

CHAPTER FOUR
GROWING THROUGH CHANGE, INNOVATION AND TRANSITION

A. INTRODUCTION
(Taken from *Ten Innovative Churches* by Elmer Towns, Regal Books, 1990, Chapter One, Managing Change for Growth)

1. _____Growth is change_____. You cannot grow without change. Until you change, you cannot grow (leaders are learners). Until your organization changes, it cannot grow. But, not all change is good (some change is for the better, other change is for the worse).

B. THREE THINGS YOU NEED TO KNOW ABOUT THE FUTURE

1. The future will not be like the _____past_____.
2. The future will not be like _____your expect_____.
3. The rate of change in the future will be _____greater_____ than in the past.

C. WHY PEOPLE RESIST CHANGE?

1. Misunderstanding – they will oppose it if they don't understand.
2. Lack of ownership – they will resist if _____not included_____.
3. Habit patterns – _____hard to break_____.
4. Change is not worth the price.
5. Threat of loss of something valuable like _____security, money or control_____.
6. _____Satisfaction_____ – they like the old ways.
7. Negative attitude toward change.
8. Lack of _____respect for leaders_____.
9. _____Tradition_____, they have never done it this way.

THE MAXWELL FORMULA FOR CHANGE
People change when:
They hurt enough to change, _____fed up_____.
They learn enough to change, _____education_____.
They receive enough to change, _____strength_____.

D. THE INGREDIENTS FOR SUCCESSFUL CHANGE

1. You must be open to change yourself, _change-agent_.
2. Create an atmosphere of trust, _reason_.
3. You build off your previous success, _track record_.
4. They trust your leadership, _confidence_.
5. You must be open to admit mistakes, _no ego problem_.
6. They must think the change is worthwhile, _value_.

E. STRATEGY FOR CHANGE (FIVE CIRCLES OF LEADERSHIP)

1. _change-agent_. Questions you must ask yourself.
   a. You are looking for _truth_.
   b. Is this idea of change God's or mine?
   c. Am I willing to pay the price?
   d. Who will I lose?
   e. "Choose who you lose." – John Maxwell

2. _Main person_. This is the one who is essential to make change happen. You must have his/her support. You are looking for _partnership_.

   You will give the **Main Person** four things:
   a. Give them _vision_.
   b. Give them _ownership_.
   c. Give them _support_.
   d. Give them _time_.

3. _Decision – makers_.

   You are looking for _influence_. They are the "movers and shakers."
   a. Know if they are positive/negative to the change.
   b. Know them individually. Who turns their crank?
   c. Know their value commitment. What turns their crank?

4. Those _most affected_ (what you want from them).

   You are looking for _involvement_.
   a. Ask for _input_.
   b. Ask for _their interest_.
   c. Allow _concession_ for their needs whenever possible.

5. _Members_.

   You are looking for their _decision_.

Two crucial factors when you want their attention:

_____ what do they need _____ ?
_____ what do they want _____ ?

THE MAXWELL RULE OF TIMING

The wrong decision at the wrong time is a ____ disaster ____.
The wrong decision at the right time is a ____ mistake ____.
The right decision at the wrong time is ____ unaccepted ____.
The right decision at the right time leads to ____ success ____.

---

6. Courage to decide.

THE TOWNS LAW OF DECISION-MAKING

You make good decisions, on good information.
You make bad decisions, on bad information.
Without any information, you make ____ lucky decisions ____.

APPLICATION QUESTIONS

1. Give an example of how change was recently introduced and resisted in the congregation you serve. What new window do you have on interpreting what happened?
2. Describe a change your church is now experiencing (or will soon). What did you learn from this presentation that can help it occur more successfully?
3. If you were teaching this same material to your pastoral staff, what one or two points would you underscore? Why?

CHAPTER FIVE
USING FAITH TO BUILD MINISTRY

A. INTRODUCTION

1. I visited the 10 largest churches in the world. I took a missions trip to discover the largest churches in the world with three leaders. John Maxwell was in that group. The results became a two-part article in *Christian Life* magazine in 1982. The churches around the world are not large because of USA reasons, i.e., management, advertising, administrative, etc. The bottom line of this study was the faith of the leader. This became my doctoral project at Fuller Theological Seminary, i.e., _The Role of the Gift of Faith in church planting and Growth_

2. The great _change-agent_ leaders in evangelicalism have faith.

3. Definition of faith is _affirming_ what God has said in His Word. "Faith is the _substance_ of things hoped for, the _evidence_ of things not seen." – Heb. 11:1

4. George Mueller had the greatest faith of those I have studied and of all who have lived since Paul.

B. WHAT FAITH WILL DO FOR YOUR MINISTRY

1. _Bold credible_ plans. You will follow God's plan for the future, "according to your faith." – Matt. 9:29

2. _Effective workable_ ministry. "Have faith in God. For verily I say unto you, that whosoever shall say to this mountain, be thou removed and be cast into the sea, and shall not doubt in his heart, but shall believe . . . he shall have whatever he saith." – Mark 11:22, 23

3. _Obedient_. The disciples could not heal and asked, "Why could we not . . .?" – Matt. 17:19. Jesus answered, "Because of your unbelief . . . if ye have faith as a grain of mustard seed." – Matt. 17:20

4. _Change-agent_. Jesus asked, "Where is your faith?" – Luke 8:25

5. _Rewarded by God_. "Without faith it is impossible to please God, for he that cometh to God must believe that He is . . . a rewarder of them that please Him." – Heb. 11:6

6. _Example_. "Remember them which hath rule over you . . . whose faith follow." – Heb. 13:7

C. WHAT HAPPENS TO MINISTRY WITHOUT FAITH?

1. _Legalistic_. "Him that is weak in faith." – Rom. 14:1

2. _Fear and intimidation_. "God has not given us a spirit of fear, but love, power, and a sound mind." – II Tim. 1:7

3. _Missed opportunity_. "Thy faith hath made thee whole." – Mark 5:34

4. _Ignorant_ of God's purpose and plan. "The word preached did not profit them, not being mixed with faith . . ." – II Tim. 4:2

D. SIX EXPRESSIONS OF FAITH

There is only one kind of faith, i.e., to affirm God's Word. But there is more than one way to express it because there is more than one benefit to our life.

1. _____Doctrinal_____ Faith. A noun, not a verb. This is an objective doctrinal statement of faith. "The faith delivered to the saints." – Jude 3
2. _____Saving_____ Faith. This faith is a verb. An act of our will based on knowledge with emotional expressions. "For by grace are ye saved through faith." – Eph. 2:8
3. _____Justifying_____ Faith. This is a non-experiential act by God whereby we are declared righteous (*ek pistis*). "Being justified by faith." – Rom. 5:1
4. _____Indwelling_____ Faith. This is the faith of Christ in us that produces a deeper-life experience. "I live by the faith of the Son of God." – Gal. 2:20
5. _____Living by_____ Faith. This is living by the principles of the Bible. "For we walk by faith." – II Cor. 5:7
6. _____Spiritual Gift of_____ Faith. This is the ability God gives to a believer to do His work (giftedness). "God hath dealt every man the measure (gift) of faith." – Rom. 12:3

E. HOW TO GROW YOUR FAITH

1. _____Pray_____. "Increase our faith." –Luke 17:5
2. _____Bible_____. "Faith cometh by hearing . . . the Word of God." – Rom. 10:17
3. _____Obedience_____. "Oh thou of little faith." – Matt. 14:31
4. _____Seeing_____ Jesus. "Looking unto Jesus, the author and finisher of our faith." – Heb. 12:2

F. THREE STEPS TO USE YOUR FAITH

1. You grow in _____faith experience_____. Faith grows as it is exercised, just as a long-distance runner gets stronger with constant exercise. "From faith to faith, as it is written, the just shall live by faith." – Rom. 1:17
2. You tell what you want to do in a faith _____expression_____. "For assuredly, I say unto you, whoever says to this mountain, 'Be removed and be cast into the sea,' and does not doubt in his heart, but believes that those things he says will come to pass, he will have whatever he says." – Mark 11:23, NKJV
3. You plan and execute a faith _____event_____. This could be a Friend Day, Teacher Recruitment Drive, or a Building Fund Campaign.

G. FIVE WAYS TO EXPRESS FAITH.

1. Say to _____a prayer list_____. "Ye have not because ye ask not." – James 4:2
2. Say to _____prayer partner_____. "If two of you shall agree on earth concerning anything that they ask, it will be done for them by my Father in heaven." – Matt. 18:19, NKJV

3. Say in ___aims and goals___.
4. Say in ___prayer request___ to the church.
5. Say at the ___altar___. In the Old Testament, people met God at the altar where a blood sacrifice brought them together. Today, we go to the church altar to demonstrate our faith in God's ability to help.

H. THE GIFT OF FAITH

There is great disagreement concerning what this gift is and what this gift accomplishes.

1. The Gift of Faith as an ___Instrument___.
   a. An enabling gift to carry out a task.
   b. Ephesians 6:17.
   c. To all believers, not just a few (passive?).
   d. Faith is affirming what God has said in His Word.
2. The Gift of Faith as ___Insight___.
   a. C. Peter Wagner.
   b. Kenneth Kinghorn.
   c. Leslie B. Flynn.
   d. What you see?
      (1) Optimistic.
      (2) Goals.
      (3) Methods/techniques.
      (4) Confident.
   e. George Barna, *The Power of Vision*.
      Definition: ___vision for ministry is a clear mental image of a preferable future, imparted by God to His chosen stewards and is based on one's accurate understanding of God, self and circumstances.___

3. The Gift of Faith or ___Intervention___.
   a. "Have faith (*Pisteu Theu*) in God, for verily I ___say___ unto you, whosoever shall, ___say___ unto this mountain, 'be thou removed, and be cast into the sea; and shall not doubt in his heart, but shall believe that those things which he ___saith___ shall come to pass; he shall have whatsoever he ___saith___.'"
      – Mark 11: 22-23
   b. God is the ___source___ of faith, the person is ___active___, and the results are ___supernatural___.
   c. Historically, this has been called the ___gift of miracles___ or the faith ___of miracles___.
   d. Formula –
      (1) During times of crisis ___fund–raising danger___.
      (2) The person is lifted out of the natural into the supernatural.
      (3) Divine certainty.

(4) Biblical goal or purpose.

(5) God responds.

I. OBSERVATIONS OF INTERVENTIONAL FAITH

1. _Interventional faith_ goes beyond the _normal instrument of faith_ that is available for Christian work in the present world.

2. Interventional faith is more than _living by faith_. – Hab. 2:4; Rom. 1:17; Gal. 3:11; Heb. 11:38; II Cor. 5:7

3. Interventional faith goes beyond the _normal biblical_ methods and principles available to the church.

4. Interventional faith is related to circumstances that lead to a _solution_ of a problem or changing circumstances.

5. Interventional faith may _solve a problem_ or alter circumstances apart from the expected flow of things.

6. Interventional faith goes _beyond the normal tools_ that Christians use in Christian service. These tools, also called "means of grace" by sacramental churches, are the influence of the Bible, the Holy Spirit's work (conviction, illumination, guiding, filling, or empowering), the influence of a godly life, the ministry gifts (preaching, teaching, counseling, etc.), the use of the church office (pastor and deacons), the use of baptism and the Lord's Table, or involvement in the church by attendance, service, and fellowship.

7. Interventional faith is _not always dependent_ upon _exact doctrine_ or mature knowledge of doctrine.

8. Interventional faith should _not be confused with holiness of life_ nor separation from sin.

9. Interventional faith seems to be related to Christian service in the church, _rather_ than to be available for the Christian to intervene in the general affairs of life.

10. Interventional faith is based on and grows out of using _faith as a vision_ and using _faith as an instrument_.

THREE VIEWS OF THE GIFT OF FAITH

NAME	INITIATION	VISION	POWER	ACCOMPLISHMENT	AVAILABLE
1. Instrumental	God	God	God	By God	To All
2. Insight	God	Person**	God	By God	To Chosen
3. Interventional	Person*	Person**	God	By God	To Chosen

*   God is the source of all Christian work, but by exercising the _gift of_ faith, the man of God senses his responsibility for church growth and uses faith to carry it out.

**   God gives a vision through his Word for all Christian work, but in the exercise of the gift of faith, the man of God perceives a particular project in time and place.

J. APPLICATIONS OF THE GIFT OF FAITH.

1. _Announce a solution_ to problems facing the ministry. Paul made statements that God would solve problems that faced him. – Acts 27:21, 22, 25
2. _Setting goals or announcing specific plans for the ministry_. First, relying on the instruments of God; second, having vision to see what God could accomplish; third, motivating God to intervene so the work will prosper.

   From our author, faith is no mere intellectual faith. It is a living and intense conviction of the supernatural which evidences in conduct. Its most characteristic effort is heroism. It is faith which "moves mountains" of difficulties and improbability. (George Barker Stevens, *The Theology of the New Testament*, Edinburgh: T. and T. Clark, 1899, p. 518.)

3. A _positive attitude_ in the ministry. "Now faith is being sure of what we hope for and being certain of what we do not see." – Heb. 11:1, NIV

4. Recognize the human factor in exercising the gift of faith.
   a. _Knowledge_.
   b. _Experience_.
   c. _Circumstance_.

K. NINETEEN CONCLUSIONS ABOUT GROWING AND USING FAITH

1. Faith is one of the primary influences on ministry.
2. Those with growing faith also have _ministries_.
3. The leaders of growing ministries have the _____.
4. Leaders can grow their ministries through the gift of faith and they can sharpen their spiritual gift of faith to be more effective. (1) There is a gift of faith; (2) it is a capacity for Christian service; (3) it grows in its effectiveness; (4) it can produce growth in ministry.
5. If leaders do not have the gift of faith, _____.
6. Leaders can increase the _____ of their spiritual gift.
7. Ministry growth is realized as the leader progresses from _____ to _____.
8. Those who use all three aspects of the gift of faith seem to have the greatest ministry growth.
9. The _____ as an instrument can be used by the leader to influence ministry growth.
10. The gift of faith can _____ in crises that face a church or ____ _____ that hinder growth.

11. Leaders do not have to express their faith in the same manner as _____ to influence the church.

12. The gift of faith can be stimulated in potential leaders by those who exercise the gift.

13. Leaders should _____ because it will not manifest itself exactly in them as it has in their teachers.

14. Announcing or asking for victories over problems or solutions to crises can be an expression of the gift of faith.

15. There is a close _____ between the leader's perception of the strength of his faith and the actual strength of his faith.

16. Leaders who properly exercise their faith when they know they are in the _____ where God wants them, will have a better opportunity to grow.

17. Leaders who express their faith with _____ will influence church growth.

18. Those who express their faith by _____ as found in the Great Commission influence ministry growth.

19. The leader who expresses faith in the _____ of Scripture will influence ministry growth.

APPLICATION QUESTIONS

1. What did you learn about faith from this presentation?
2. Describe what Dr. Towns means by "interventional faith." To what extent do you agree or disagree with him?
3. How have the key influencers of your church seen your own faith in the last two weeks? How do you feel about the model you are setting?
4. What is the next step you need to take in growing and using faith? What might the results be if God blessed it above what you could ask or think?

CHAPTER SIX
TYPES OF DOUBT

The deeper Christian life (EX – 2) should be a constant motivation to the believer as he goes through prosperity or trials. The inner assurance and his relationship keep him close in his walk with God. But, as the Christian begins to drift from God, inward changes are not always manifested with outward signs. The Christian continues to practice the outward forms of fellowship, yet they become _meaningless in his spiritual life_.

> Drifting usually causes little outward change, but is a _slow subtle process_.

Just as there are steps of faith in which a believer grows in his relationship with God, there also seems to be descending steps away from faith. The _possibility of growth_ in one's Christian walk allows for a _possible downward spiral_ away from trust in the Lord. The following five categories of unbelief (UF = the Unbelief of Faith) are not hierarchical concerning one's descent from God, yet they differ in their _intensity and ability_ to weaken the Christian's faith in God.

> ### CATEGORIES OF UNBELIEF
> UF – 1 Weak faith
> UF – 2 Little faith
> UF – 3 Faithlessness
> UF – 4 Doubt
> UF – 5 Unbelief

UF – 1: Weak Faith

The first step away from confidence in God is the weakened faith of a believer.

> "And not being weak in faith, he did not consider his own body, already dead (since he was about a hundred years old), and the deadness of Sarah's womb." – Romans 4:19

Theology of Weak Faith:

1. Two different Greek words are used for the idea of "weak faith."
   a. *Adunatos* – meaning "_without power_."
   b. *Asthenes* – meaning "without strength."

2. A person with UF – 1 weak faith gets his eyes off Jesus Christ and becomes _____ _____more concerned with legalism_____ (what to eat, wear, and do).

3. Those who claim the experience of walking with God, yet base it on _____ _self-denials, special diets, and clothes_____, do not have strong faith, but are weak in faith.

> "Do not destroy the work of God for the sake of food. All things indeed are pure, but it is evil for the man who eats with offense." – Romans 14:20

The person who is weak in faith lacks the spiritual power to accomplish what he attempts for God and also lacks the _strength to endure in the trial of faith_____.

UF – 2: Little Faith

On several occasions, Jesus described His disciples as having "little faith," especially when they were _not able to serve God the way they wanted_____.
As John Gill notes, "They lacked in moments of anxiety the courage which leads men to rely implicitly on the love and wisdom of their father."

> Little faith is a mix of _faith and doubt_____.

Theology of Little Faith:

1. Trying to serve God with _one's own ability_____ and not in the power of Christ.

2. Little faith could include serving God with the wrong motivation, wrong tools, or trying to serve God _out of ignorance_____.

3. "Little faith" was a term used by rabbinical teachers to identify those who at _____ _times doubted_____.

4. From the expressions of Christ towards His disciples, it is evident that the disciples had _some faith_____, for they asked Jesus to help them.

> "And immediately Jesus stretched out His hand and caught him, and said to him, 'O you of little faith, why did you doubt?'" – Matthew 14:31

UF – 3: Faithlessness

The Christian who experiences faithlessness _has sinned_____ and must return to the deeper Christian life.

Theology of Faithlessness:

1. Faithlessness is a Christian's _unwillingness to trust God_, even in the face of evidence.

> "And when they had come to the multitude, a man came to Him, kneeling down to Him and saying, 'Lord, have mercy on my son, for he is an epileptic and suffers severely; for he often falls into the fire and often into the water. So I brought him to Your disciples, but they could not cure him.' Then Jesus answered and said, 'O faithless and perverse generation, how long shall I be with you? How long shall I bear with you? Bring him here to Me.' And Jesus rebuked the demon, and it came out of him; and the child was cured from that very hour. Then the disciples came to Jesus privately and said, 'Why could we not cast it out?'" – Matthew 17:14-19

2. *Faithless* come from the Greek term *apistis* meaning "unbelief." The Greek word *pistis* means "faith," and the prefix *a* is a means of _negating or neutralizing faith_.

3. Faithlessness means, "_"no faith" or "neutral faith"_".

4. This is not _negative distrust of God_, the individual simply does not believe, nor disbelieve God. The person is _neutral_.

5. The faithless believer has denied the experience of _walking with God_.

> "So he said to them, 'Unless I see in His hands the print of the nails, and put my finger into the print of the nails, and put my hand into His side, I will not believe.'" – John 20:25

UF – 4: Doubt

Instead of living by faith, and being obedient to the Word of God, the doubting believer begins to think through the nonscriptural options. He allows _his reason to be controlled by his unbelief_, not the Word of God.

Theology of Doubt:

1. The Greek word *dialogia* is translated "doubt," meaning "_to reason through_."

> "I desire therefore that the men pray everywhere, lifting up holy hands, without wrath and doubting." – 1 Timothy 2:8

2. The Christian experiencing UF – 4 is no longer experiencing fellowship with Christ because doubt is _controlling his thought processes_.

3. Doubt is usually a ___slow process___, which does not always include outward sin.

4. This experience will ultimately lead to ___life corrupting sin___.

UF – 5: Unbelief

"Unbelief is the ___negative expression___ of rejection by the Christian of the existence of God, the Word of God, and/or the claims of God in his life." (53)

Theology of Unbelief:

1. The Christian has come to the point were he is beyond a passive relationship with God to the extent that ___negative expression he refuses to believe___

> "The trouble of unbelief is always in the heart, the seat of the will." – R. C. H. Lenski

2. Unbelief manifests itself when the believer refuses to follow the ___Commands of God___ (spiritual disciplines, etc.), or commits deliberate sins.

3. The Christian who experiences unbelief does not lose his salvation, but loses his ___fellowship with God___.

> "Immediately the father of the child cried out and said with tears, 'Lord, I believe; help my unbelief!'" – Mark 9:24

4. Unbelief is the ___opposite experience___ of the deeper Christian life.

CHAPTER SEVEN
PLANNING FOR EVANGELISM
BUT GETTING REVIVAL

A. INTRODUCTION

1. Churches have grown when God pours revival out on His people and their renewed spirit reaches out to the community, producing:
   a. _Internal growth_ within individuals and churches.
   b. _External growth_.
   c. _Biological growth_ growth. — small church
   d. _Transfer_ growth. — large church
   e. _Conversion_ growth. — medium church

2. There are many evangelistic crusades where souls are won to Christ while churches do not experience revival (but some individuals experience internal revival). But when there is true revival from God, souls will be won to Christ, and the church grows.

B. WHAT IS REVIVAL?

1. What a revival is not:
   a. Revival is not an _evangelistic crusade_.
   b. Revival is not a _meeting_.
   c. Revival is not just a _feeling of excitement_.

2. Bible words for revival:
   a. Revival (Latin) means, "return to life."
      (1) Return to _New Testament Christianity_.
      (2) Return to the commitment and joy of _your conversion_.
   b. *Chayah* – a revival that restores life.
   c. *Michyah* – a revival that preserves life.
   d. *Anazao* – a revival renews life.
   e. *Anazopero* – a revival that rekindles life.

3. Definition of revival. Revival is an outpouring of God's presence on His people when Christians:
   a. _Repent_ of sin.
   b. _Renew_ their love to God.
   c. _Recommit_ themselves to God's purposes.
   d. Invest extended time in prayer, communion with God, meditation and,
   e. Experience blessings in _Christian service_.

4. Verses of revival:

> "When the times of refreshing shall come from the presence of the Lord." –Acts 3:19
>
> "I will pour out My Spirit on all flesh." – Acts 2:17
>
> "If My people, which are called by My name, shall humble themselves, and pray, and seek My face, and turn from their wicked ways; then will I hear from heaven, and will forgive their sin, and will heal their land." – II Chronicles 7:14

C. *THE TEN GREATEST REVIVALS EVER*
(Taken from the book *The Ten Greatest Revivals Ever*, by Elmer Towns and Douglas Porter, Servant Publications, Ann Arbor, Michigan, 2000 A.D.)

1. The ten greatest revivals ever:
   The 1904 Revival beginning in Wales
   The Great Awakening, 1727 1750
   The Second Great Awakening, 1780 – 1810
   The General Awakening, 1830 – 1840
   The Layman's Prayer Revival, 1857 – 1861
   The World War II Revival, 1935 – 1950
   The Baby Boomer Revival, 1965 – 1975
   The Pre-Reformation Revivals, 1300-1500
   The Protestant Reformation, 1517
   Pentecost, the Beginning of Revival, A.D. 30

2. How the ten were chosen:
   a. Was it an isolated event (meetings or places) or a revival that sprang up ____ *or did it involve the larger body of Christ*? "I will pour out My Spirit on all flesh." – Acts 2:17
   b. Did it fit the ___*biblical   guidelines*___ of revival, i.e., definition?
   c. Was there a demonstration of ___*God's presence*___?

   > Don't seek the hand of God in miracles,
   > See the heart of God in intimacy.

   d. Was ___*the church*___ awakened to its New Testament task?

> "It is by revivals of religion that the church of God makes its most visible advance. When all things seem becalmed, when no breath stirs the air, when the sea is like lead and the sky is low and gray, when all worship seems to have ended but the worship of matter, then it is that the Spirit of God is poured upon the church, then it is then the Christianity of the apostles and martyrs, not that of the philosophers and liberals, keeps rising – as Vinet says – from the catacombs of oblivion, and appears young and fresh in the midst of the obsolete things of yesterday and the day before." – Sir William Robertson Nicoll

e. Was culture/society ___positively influenced___?
f. Are there ___reliable sources___ that demonstrate the greatness of the revival?

3. Analysis of the ten greatest revivals

The 1904 Revival

Persons: Evan Roberts at ___Wales___.
Places: William Seymore at ___Azusa Street___.
Manchuria, Korea, Mizoram, India

> "The (1904 Awakening) is the farthest reaching revival of the movements of general awakenings, for it affected the whole of the evangelical course in India, Korea and China, renewed revivals in Japan, South Africa, and sent an awakening over Africa, Latin America, and the South Seas." – J. Edwin Orr

Results:
a. Founding of ___Pentecostal denominations___.
b. Temperance Movement.
c. Impetus of worldwide ___missionary endeavors___.
d. Beginning of interdenominational agencies and strategy.

The Great Awakening, 1727 – 1750

Persons: Count Von Zinzendorf, Herrnhut, Austria.
John Wesley, the Evangelical Awakening of ___England___
George Whitefield, Revival in England and America.
Jonathan Edwards, ___New England___
Moravian Watch Night Revival of Fetter Lane, December 31, 1731.

Results:
a. Founding of religious universities and colleges in America.
b. Birth to the Sunday School Movement.
c. Initiated literacy among the masses.
d. Gave congregations a voice in their affairs and thrust laymen into areas of ministries.

e. Kept "French" spirit of _lawlessness_ from England and America.

f. Infusion of _democracy_ into the American colonies, laying the foundation for the American Revolution.

The Second Great Awakening, 1780 – 1810

Persons: Peter Cartwright, _Cane Ridge_, Kentucky, 1800
            Timothy Dwight, Yale College Revival
            Asahel Nettleton, Bridgewater Revival of New England
            Haldane Brothers, Geneva's _Second Revival_

Results:

a. _New Evangelistic Associations_, i.e., British and Foreign Bible Society, Religious Tract Society, London Missionary Society, Church Missionary Society.

b. Itinerary _Preaching_.

c. Growth of lay preachers.

d. Growth of _Brush Arbor meetings (camp meetings)_.

The General Awakening, 1830 – 1840

Person: Charles Finney, the _Rochester Revival_.
           Titus Coan, The Hawaiian Revival

> His weeping was so loud, and his trembling so great, that the whole congregation was moved as by a common sympathy. Many wept aloud, and many commenced praying together. The scene was such as I had never before witnessed. I stood dumb in the midst of this weeping, wailing, praying multitude, not being able to make myself heard for about twenty minutes.

          The Mississippi Valley Enterprise, 1829
          William Burns, Kilsyth Anniversary Revival, Scotland

> "There have been instances in the history of the Church when the telling and retelling of the wonderful works of God have been used to rekindle the expectations of the faithful intercessors and prepare the way for another awakening." – J. Edwin Orr

Results:

a. Abolition of worldwide _African slave trade_.

b. Improved _working conditions_ of the masses.

c. Rapid expansion of American _Sunday school movement_.

d. Founding of religious hospitals, asylums, orphanages, and schools.

The Laymen's Prayer Revival, 1857 – 1861

Persons: Phoebe Palmer, Hamilton, Ontario, 1857
Dwight L. Moody, The _Illinois Band_ 1861.
Jeremiah Lanphier, The Fulton Street prayer meeting, New York.
Jamaican Revival.
James McQuilkin, Ulster, Ireland.

Results:
a. The use of _organized evangelistic_ crusades.
b. Focus on _prayer_ (without preaching) for revival.
c. Use of _media_ (newspapers) to spread news of revival.
d. Use of tents _for revivals_.

The World War II Revival 1935 – 1950

Persons: J. Edwin Orr, The New Zealand Revival.
Billy Graham, The _Los Angeles Crusade_.
Duncan Campbell, The Lewis Awakening, New Hebrides, _Scotland_.

Results:
a. Great numbers of WWII soldiers _went to the mission field_.
b. New wave of Bible colleges and institutions.
c. Use of media to evangelize.

The Baby Boomer Revival, 1965 – 1970

Persons: Chuck Smith, The _Jesus People_ Revival.
Asbury College Revival.
Independent Baptist Revival.
The Canadian Prairie Revival.

Results:
a. Pentecostalism and Charismatic Movement moved into _____
main-line denominations.
b. Introduction of _praise music_ into worship expression.
c. The introduction of the _bus_ movement.
d. Emergence of Yonggi Cho and the _cell movement_.
e. Application of _church growth_ principles to evangelism.

The Pre-Reformation Revival, 1300 – 1500

Persons: John Wycliffe, 1382, _Lollards_.
John Hus, 1415, Bohemia.
Savonarola, 1481, Florence, Italy.

Results:
These were _a shining light_ to the power of God during the
Dark Ages.

Called ___*for reforms*___ because of the corruption and abuse of the Roman Church.

Began circulating/preaching ___*Scriptures*___ to the people.

The Reformation, 1517

Persons: Martin Luther, 1517, _____.
          Ulrich Zwingli, 1522, Zurich, Switzerland.
          John Calvin, 1541, _____, Switzerland.

Results:

a. The establishment of a _____.
b. Translated the Bible into _____.
c. The desire for "_____" as opposed to be governed by Rome.
d. The reorganization of _____of Europe.
e. Took strength from the _____ and gave impetus back to the emergence of science, arts, culture, and spread of Western civilization.

Pentecost, A.D. 30

Persons: Peter, and later Paul.

4. Anointed methods and the ten greatest revivals:

   1. 1904 WALES REVIVAL: balanced.
   2. THE FIRST GREAT AWAKENING: _____, Sunday School _____.
   3. THE SECOND GREAT AWAKENING: _____, Brush Arbor preaching.
   4. THE GENERAL AWAKENING: _____, Anxious Seat.
   5. THE LAYMAN PRAYER REVIVAL: tents, evangelistic crusades, _____.
   6. THE WORLD WAR II REVIVAL: _____, media, _____.
   7. THE BABY BOOMER REVIVAL: _____, small groups, _____, confession.
   8. PRE-REFORMATION REVIVALS: _____.
   9. THE REFORMATION: _____, self-rule, new political forces from religious impetus.
   10. PENTECOST A.D. 30: the foundation of the above.

5. What can be learned from methods?
   a. A person with the anointing of God successfully uses a method, which makes it appear God ___*has anointed the method*___.

> Methods are many,
> Principles are few.
> Methods may change,
> But principles never do.

   b. Just as people can lose their anointing when they turn from God, so a method can lose ___*its effectiveness*___.
   c. Don't look to a method for effectiveness in ministry, ___*look to God*___.

6. Descriptions of revival:
   a. Revival is an experience, i.e., ___*atmosphere*___ revival.
   b. Revival is a ___*work of God*___. Jonathan Edwards taught that a revival is the sovereign outpouring of God. People could do nothing to instigate a revival.
   c. Revival involves a ___*work of man*___.

> "The appropriate means could bring revival to God's people, i.e., prayer, repentance, tarrying, seeking God, etc. I said that a revival is the result of the right use of the appropriate means, the means, which God has enjoined for the production of a revival. Otherwise, God would not have enjoined them. But means will not produce a revival, we all know, without the blessing of God. No more will grain when it is sown, produce a crop without the blessing of God. It is impossible for us to say that there is not as direct an influence or agency from God, to produce a crop of grain, as there is to produce a revival." – Charles Finney (1835)

   d. Revival can include a total area (geography, denomination, or group of churches) or a selective area. (selected churches in an area).
   e. Revival is atmospheric (group) or individual (internal).
   f. Americans use the word *revival*, while church history and churches outside America use the word ___*awakening*___.
   g. The outpouring of the Holy Spirit (usually ___*group oriented*___).

> "An evangelical awakening is a movement of the Holy Spirit bringing about a revival of New Testament Christianity in the church of Christ and its related community. Such an awakening may change in a significant way an individual only; or district, or the whole body of believers throughout a country or a continent; or indeed the large body of believers throughout the world. The outpouring of the Spirit affects the reviving of the church, the awakening of the masses, and the movement of uninstructed people toward the Christian faith; the revived church, by many or by few, is moved to engage in evangelism, in teaching, and in social action." – J. Edwin Orr

h. The anointing of the Holy Spirit also called the filling of the Holy Spirit, usually refers to ___Individuals___.

i. The manifestations during revival, i.e., phenomena.

    a. Samples include "slain in the spirit," jerking, shouting, barking, dancing in the spirit, etc.

    b. When the divine is poured into the human, expect the human to react in ___unusual ways___.

    c. Some manifestations are ___sprinkled___ throughout history.

    d. Some of the greatest revivals ___do not record manifestations___, some of the greatest revivals had them.

    e. If you measure ___the success___ of a revival by its manifestations, you miss the point of revival.

    f. Don't seek the extraordinary signs of a revival, ___seek God___.

> "Since the days of Pentecost there is no record of the sudden and direct work of the Spirit of God upon the souls of men that has not been accompanied by events more or less abnormal. It is, indeed, one consideration, only natural that is should be so. We cannot expect an abnormal inrush of divine light and power, so profoundly affecting the emotions and changing the lives of men, without remarkable results. As well expect a hurricane, an earthquake, or a flood, to leave nothing abnormal in its course, as to expect a true revival that is not accompanied by events quite out of our ordinary experience." – A. T. Schofield

j. An anointed method is for a ___specific time and place___.
When conditions change, "new methods" will usually be used by God.

D. THE NINE CONTEMPORARY EXPRESSIONS OF REVIVAL

(Taken from the book, *Rivers of Revival*, by Neil Anderson and Elmer Towns, Regal Books, Ventura, CA, 1998)

1. ___Evangelism___. (Billy Graham)
Revival will come when the church places soul winning in its primary place and wins (enough) people to Christ (to make a difference).

2. ___Repentance___. (Jerry Falwell)
Revival will come when the church calls its members and society to repent of its sins, i.e., the sins that people commit that are barriers to revival. – II Chronicles 7:14

3. ___Deeper Life___. (Henry Blackaby)
Revival will come when God's people will get closer to Christ, i.e., the deeper Christian life. (The crucified life, abiding life, abundant life, etc.).

4. ___Prayer Movement___. (Ed Silvoso)
Revival will come when God's people pray.
   a. Prayer ___walking___: praying on site with insight.
   b. ___Blessing the unsaved___: i.e., the goodness of God leads to repentance.
   c. Praying through the 10 – 40 window.
   d. Thirty denomination–wide prayer initiatives.
   e. "See you at the pole," originally a Southern Baptist church program.
   f. Prayer Summits. Clergy are going away to pray for 2 or 3 days. No speaking or seminars, just prayer. Begun by Joe Aldridge, President of Multnoma Bible College.
   g. City-wide prayer events. March for Jesus, concerts of prayer rallies, etc.
   h. National prayer gatherings. Bill Bright and others called for a conference on prayer and fasting. Four thousand people came to "not eat," but pray. Eight major events went on at one time in the Los Angeles Civic Center with 90 nations represented.
   i. U. S. Prayer Directory. Ten years ago there was no directory of prayer movements. Now it has 70 pages listing organizations committed to prayer, all groups from Pentecostals to Presbyterians, from Episcopalians to Baptists.
   j. New Christian magazines devoted to prayer.
   k. A simultaneous nation-wide prayer meeting when 1000 radio stations dedicated three hours to prayer May 4, 1996, and October 21, 1996.
   l. At the National Consultation on Evangelism, December 7, 1997, it was discovered five people are publishing books with the phrase in the title, *The Coming Revival*. Of course, Bill Bright was the first.

5. Removing ___territorial spirits___ (C. Peter Wagner). Revival or evangelism cannot come to our area because there are territorial spirits, which control the hearts and minds of the inhabitants. Spiritual mapping helps to:
   a. Determine the spirit.
   b. The power (addiction or infliction) by which he controls, and
   c. The path to the spirit's removal. *Breaking Strongholds In Your City,* (Regal Books, 1993).

6. Removing ___the curse___ (John Dawson, President, Youth With A Mission). Because of past sins, there is a curse upon people groups that make them resistant to revival or evangelism. The curse can be removed by:
   a. Identificational ___repentance___.
   b. Confession of sins of fathers who originated the curse. *Healing America's Wounds* (Regal Books, 1994).

7. Freedom ___from addiction___ (Neil Anderson). A church or individual may be under bondage so that revival or evangelism is not possible. Anderson teaches "Truth Encounter," not a "Demon Encounter" or "Curse Encounter." He teaches seven steps to "Freedom in Christ."

a. Counterfeit vs. Revival, "I renounce."
b. Deception vs. Truth, "I recognize."
c. Bitterness vs. Forgiveness, "I forgive."
d. Rebellion vs. Submission, "I submit."
e. Pride vs. Humility, "I humble."
f. Bondage vs. Freedom, "I renounce."
g. Acquiesce vs. Renunciation, "I reject."

Setting Your Church Free (Regal Books, 1994) or *Victory Over The Darkness* (Regal Books, 1990)

8. ___Worship Encounter___ (Jack Hayford). To lead people to experience the fullness of God's presence as they worship Him in spirit and truth. Revival is not available until God's presence is felt among His people. *Worship His Majesty*, by Jack Hayford, Regal Books, 2000 A.D.

9. ___Holy Spirit Encounter___: revival comes when powerless believers experience the fullness of the Holy Spirit so they can release revival through the church into the world.

E. CAN REVIVAL BE INITIATED BY MAN?

1. The "___great apostasy___" argument. There will never be another great revival before the coming of Christ.

2. The "___God is sovereign___" argument. Revivals only come from God; man does not have a role in causing a revival.

3. The "___pray and hope___" argument. People can pray and wait for a revival, but there is no automatic guarantee that it will come.

4. The law of ___sowing and reaping___. When people use the appropriate means in the correct way, God will honor His Word and pour out revival.

5. The nature of <u>conditional promises</u>. God will pour out revival only when people meet God's conditions.

F. WHAT ARE THE CONDITIONS OF AN OUTPOURING OF THE HOLY SPIRIT?

1. Invite "___carriers of revival___" to create an appetite for revival. These come from where the fire of God is burning, they bring illustrations, testimonies and methods that begin a fire/revival in places where they visit.
2. ___Desire___ – Isaiah 44:3
3. Prayer – Zech. 10:1; cf. Joel 2:23; James 5:7
4. ___Repentance___ – Prov. 1:23; Isa. 57:15

5. Lordship of Christ – cf. Isa. 32:15; Joel 2:27, 29; Acts 2:17, 18,36
6. _Fellowship_ – Psalm 133
7. Worship – Psalm 22:3, 50:23; II Chron. 5:13,14
8. Financial stewardship – Mal. 3:10
9. Absolute _Surrender_ .

CHAPTER EIGHT
WORSHIP

> **WORSHIP:**
> Worship is recognizing who God is and giving God His worth-ship.

A. WHAT IS WORSHIP?

(Taken from the book, *Putting An End To Worship Wars*, by Elmer Towns, Broadman and Holman, Nashville, Tennessee, 1997. This book is available in its entirety online at www.elmertowns.com).

Churches grow because people experience the presence of God as they worship Him corporately and individually. We are to sacrifice to God four things:
1. _Lives_
2. _Thanksgiving_
3. Praise (Hebrew 13)
4. Service to others

1. Worship in the Old Testament.
   a. Man was created for _worship_ and _rulership_. – Rev. 4:11; Gen. 1:26
   b. Worship demands fallen man _sacrifice_ on the altar to God. –I Sam. 15:22; Heb. 13:15
   c. Worship produces power to release people from _bondage_.
   d. The Jewish calendar revolves around worship, as is evidenced by the _festivals_

2. New Testament vocabulary of worship.
   a. *Proskuneo* – (literally means "to kiss the hand.") Making obeisance, paying homage, doing _reverence_ to God.
   b. *Sebomai/Sembazonmai* – the feeling of _awe_ or devotion inspired by worship. –cf. Acts 13:42, 50; 17:4, 17
   c. *Latreuo* – worship as a _service_ to God. –Acts 13
   d. *Eusebeo* – showing _honor_ toward one who should be honored. –Acts 17:23; cf. I Tim. 5:4 – translated here "piety").

3. Worship and personality.
   a. Worship begins with a _face to face_ encounter with God.
   b. Worship stirs the _heart_ based upon biblical facts.
   c. Worship affects the _worshipper_ as a person magnifies God for what He is.

> God dwells in the <u>praises of His people</u>.

B. WARREN BIRD'S TOP TEN REASONS TO WORSHIP

(From *Into the Future*, Elmer Towns and Warren Bird, page 153)

1. Worship results in a Christian taking better care of _the earth_.
2. Worship increases the Christian's vision of the _greatness of God_.
3. Worship is something _God desires_ from His children.
4. Worship is what seems to happen whenever _the Holy Spirit_ shows up.
5. Worship of God helps defeat the _second greatest power_ in the universe.
6. Worship puts a Christian's life into _perspective_.
7. Worship is what a Christian will _do for all of eternity_; it is the main activity of heaven.
8. Worship stirs a Christian's _evangelistic passion_.
9. Worship is at _the center of everything_ the church believes, practices, and seeks to accomplish.
10. Worship is unavoidable for _the growing christian_.

C. WHAT IS THE WORSHIP SERVICE?

> According to a survey conducted by George Barna, "one-third of the adults who regularly attend Christian church services say that they have never experienced God's presence at any time during their life." In addition to this, seven of ten adults (71 percent) say they have never experienced God's presence at a church service. (From *Into the Future*, Elmer Towns and Warren Bird, pages 133, 154)

A worship service is convened (1) to _serve God_ with our praise and (2) to _serve people's needs_ with His sufficiency, i.e., worship His majesty.

1. Our service to God in worship.
   a. We must _assemble_ ourselves together. – Heb. 10:25
   b. Then we worship God _corporately_ through such activities as singing unto the Lord. – Psalm 96:1
   c. Continuing in prayer.
   d. Sharing.
   e. The apostles' doctrine – Acts 2:42

2. Meeting people's needs through worship.
   Worship meets the needs of the worshiper by inviting the _very presence of God_ in the midst of the worshipping body allowing God Himself to meet their needs.

D. HOW TO WORSHIP GOD

In John 4:24, Jesus states that, "God is Spirit, and those who worship Him must worship in spirit and truth." The two aspects, spirit and truth, must always go together. You cannot truly worship God if you separate the two. *Spirit* is the __*way in which*__ you worship; your heart's attitude towards God. *Truth* is the __*right content*__; being grounded in correct biblical doctrine.

1. We worship God with our regenerated __*spirit*__. – John 4:23
2. We worship God with our renewed __*mind*__. – Phil. 2:5; Rom. 12:2; I Cor. 14:15; Psalm 47:6, 7
3. We worship God with our revived __*emotions*__. – Col. 2:23; Psalm 46:1; 100:1
4. We worship God with our ready __*will / volition*__. – Rom. 12:1
5. We worship God with our rededicated __*body*__. – Rom. 12:1; Phil. 2:9, 10; Mic. 6:6-8; Psalm 63:3,4; 149:3

> "God is most glorified in me when I am most satisfied in him." – John Piper

E. KEEPING WORSHIP IN THE WORSHIP SERVICE

Though worship is something that can be done at anytime and anywhere, it is important that the worship service conducted every week be a true time of worship to God. The four following principles will help ensure that each and every worship service is truly a time when God is given His worth-ship.

1. __*Preparation*__ – failing to prepare is preparing to fail.
   a. Center the worship service on a specific aim.
   b. Gather the materials for the worship service.

2. __*Examination*__ – seeing God causes us to see ourselves.
   a. Isaiah in the Temple – Isa. 6:1-13
   b. Moses before the burning bush – Ex. 3:1-17
   c. Worship through the Communion Table – Matt. 26:20-30
   d. Paul's experience on the Damascus Road – Acts 9:1-9

3. __*Expectation*__ – "My soul, wait silently for God alone, For my expectation is from Him." – Psalm 62:5
   a. Appropriation.
   b. __*Meditation*__.
   c. __*Consummation*__.
   d. Worship is the deepest experience in life.
   e. "And you will seek Me and find Me, when you search for Me with all your heart." – Jeremiah 29:13

4. __*Transformation*__.
   In a true worship experience, a person examines himself in light of a meeting with God. He expects God to do for him what only God can do. He then

appropriates the power and person of the Lord for his life. Through deep meditation he dedicates his life. His life is transformed.

Worship never allows us to remain the same person because it impacts us in several ways: (From *Into the Future*, Elmer Towns and Warren Bird, pages 131-135)

1. _Heart response_ – true worship comes from the heart
2. _Transformed life_ – we deepen our relationship with God.
3. _Raised ante_ – a greater sacrifice from the worshiper.
4. _Changed environment_ – true worship gives new meaning and new forms of expression.

F. PHYSICAL MANIFESTATIONS OF WORSHIP

Manifestation

Because God is infinite (all-powerful, and all-glorious) and because man is finite (limited), when deity fills humanity, man cannot contain God and man wants to share the glory he has received: so he manifests the power and glory of God in many different ways (jerks, crying, laughing, slain in the Spirit, shouting, running, etc.). Some manifestations are expressed in all revivals. However, man should never seek the manifestation or glory in the manifestation; rather, man should glory in God who is the source of all blessing.

G. WORSHIP AND CHURCH GROWTH

1. People basing their choice of a local church on its _worship expressions_.
2. Churches using various worship expressions as a means to _evangelism_.
3. Expressions of worship can be studied to determine its _effectiveness_.
4. New denominations are being formed around methodology _worship expressions_.

H. WORSHIP AS A CHOICE

1. Worship is like a car. Although an automobile is _basic transportation_, it is chosen because of the owner's needs, personality, ethnic background, purpose, etc.

2. Historically people choose a new local church on:
   a. _Doctrine_.
   b. The name of the church.
   c. _Denomination_.

3. Now, people choose a new local church on _style of worship_.
   a. Consumerism is the engine that drives American society.
   b. Church worshipers as _consumers_.

c. Worship menus are not filled with doctrinal options but _worship options_.

4. Six areas of tension in worship
(Taken from Elmer Towns and Warren Bird, *Into the Future*, page 135)
   a. Seeker sensitivity vs. _edified Christians_.
   - Is your congregation using its worship services to value lost people and help them find Christ?
   b. _Human - centered_ vs. God-centered
      1) What happens when increased emphasis is placed on _God's concern_ for "my" cares and concerns?
      2) Ask yourself, "What did _God_ get out of the service?"
   c. _Dumbing down_ vs. shaping up
      1) When worship focuses so heavily on solving the problems of life, we may fail to lift people up to _God's level_.
      2) Do we accommodate the worst in popular culture, lowering standards to meet people where they are at the expense of _lifting people to where they should be_?
   d. Conforming to the world vs. _transforming_ the world
      1) To what extent should current movies, television shows, or hit songs be referenced or used in worship?
      2) Behind this topic lies the issue of _conforming_ to the world versus _transforming it_.
   e. _Egotism_ vs. community
      1) Should one person raise their hands, while another claps; one person sits as another stands?
      2) Some believe that to please God most, the congregation should do _everything together_; sing together, pray the Lord's Prayer together, read Scripture together, etc.
   f. Institutional Event vs. _Individual_ Event
      - Is worship a group event or does it take _people individually_ to God?

I. STYLES OF WORSHIP AND MINISTRY

> "All worship services are contemporary to *some* generation, but most are 'contemporary' to an era other than today." – George Hunter

"Probably the most emotional discussions concern musical style used in worship. For example, in discussing some of the newer music used in churches, one prominent American pastor remarked:

There are several reasons for opposing it. One, it's too new. Two, its often worldly, even blasphemous. The new Christian music is not as pleasant as the more established style because there are so many new songs, you can't learn them all. It also puts too much emphasis on instrumental music rather than on godly lyrics. This new music creates disturbances, making people act indecently and disorderly. The preceding generation got along without it.'"

Those words were voiced in ___*1723*___. They were a critique of Isaac Watts, who produced the first hymnbook in the English language . . ." (From *Into the Future*, Elmer Towns and Warren Bird, page 134)

1. Historically two basic worship styles in Protestant church
   a. ___*High church*___.
   b. ___*Low church*___.

2. Liturgical worship
   a. ___*Invocation*___
   b. ___*Doxology*___
   c. Lord's Prayer
   d. Choir anthems
   e. Responsive reading of scripture
   f. Pastoral prayer
   g. Gloria Patri
   h. Singing ___*"amen" at end of each hymn*___

3. Congregational church
   a. Brethren of the common life
   b. Anabaptists
   c. Mennonites
   d. Moravians
   e. Puritans
   f. Pilgrims
   g. Style:
      ▪ Preaching was ___*emotional*___.
      ▪ Songs expressed ___*deep emotion*___.
      ▪ Testimonies
      ▪ Prayers from ___*laymen*___.

> "It's [worship] an inward quality, and not an external thing. So musical style, skill, and new techniques are not the most important considerations." – LaMar Boschman

J. SIX WORSHIP PARADIGMS

1. ___*Evangelistic*___
2. ___*Bible – expositional*___
3. ___*Renewal*___
4. ___*Body-life / cell church*___

5. _Liturgical_
6. _Congregational_

K. WHY NOW?

1. All six qualities have been embryonic in every true church since Pentecost.

2. Interstate and Internet:
   a. The interstate freeway – represents explosion of _transportation_ since World War II
   b. The Internet – reflects explosion of modern _communication_

L. NEW MODELS FOR REACHING VARIOUS AGE GROUPS

1. _Seeker-centered or seeker-driven_
   a. Focus – _unchurched_, irreligious people
   b. Biblical precedent – "seek and save what was lost." – Luke 19:10
   c. Example – Willow Creek Community Church, Pastor Bill Hybels

2. _Seeker-sensitive_
   a. Focus – speaks primarily to _Christians_, with a sensitivity to the unchurched guests
   b. Biblical precedent – sermons in Acts where Christians and non-Christians were present
   c. Example – Saddleback Community Church, Pastor Rick Warren

3. _Blended_
   a. Focus – combines _two different philosophies_ of ministry to reach two target audiences, often an older and a younger one
   b. Biblical precedent – Jerusalem Council, adjusting to include Gentiles – Acts 15
   c. Example – Southeast Christian Church, Pastor Bob Russell

4. _Multiple-track_
   a. Focus – different _service times_ with distinct approaches to worship
   b. Biblical precedent – "become all things to all people." – I Cor. 9:19-23
   c. Example – Church of the Resurrection, Pastor Adam Hamilton

M. SPIRITUAL MOTIVES

1. Explosion of interest in spiritual gifts.
2. A specific gift holds worship and ministry together.
3. _Gift colonization_: people choose a church where their personal dominant gift is also the dominant corporate gift.
4. _Gift gravitation_: people moving to a church where their gift is exercised.

5. _____Gift assimilation_____: new members assimilate the dominant gifts of the church they attend.

N. OBSERVATIONS ABOUT WORSHIP

1. Some have the same worship experience but express themselves with different _____forms_____.
2. Worship is legitimate when _____God_____ is its focus. Expressions of worship are not hierarchical but express a range of emotions.
3. The strengths of each worship are found in the other worship expressions.
4. No single worship experience has a _____corner on the market_____.
5. Reflections of worship may characterize _____different times_____ in a person's life.
6. Worship experiences become _____standardized when_____ similar needs gravitate and colonize together.
7. Churches from the same denomination may be found in all six worship experiences.
8. _____Little_____ correlation between experience and doctrine.
9. No one type of worship meets _____all needs_____ of all members.
10. Some begin at one experience and gravitate.
11. Some are converted within one worship experience and _____remain_____.
12. When moving geographically, it is best to seek a church that will maximize _____your strengths_____.
13. Believers in a worship experience that have different expectations recognize what they can do rather than _____complain_____.
14. Since different worship presents problems, don't emphasize our differences, but _____our unity_____.
15. Some express their worship differently; we are not _____obligated_____ to follow their worship.
16. Because most want to keep the worship traditions, they _____fight change_____.
17. Be wary of the _____elitists_____ who reject worship that is different from his or her own.
18. Worship wars break out because leaders have not taught people _____how to worship_____.

O. CONCLUSION

1. The effectiveness of worship is not measured by _____atmosphere_____.
2. True worship is always measured by the response of _____the believer's heart to God_____.
3. True worship is measured by the transformation of the worshipers.
4. True worship never allows us to _____remain the same person_____.
5. True worship involves change and it also includes that which _____never changes_____.
6. Types (styles) of worship are not _____right or wrong_____.

CHAPTER NINE
FASTING FOR PERSONAL BREAKTHROUGH AND CHURCH REVIVAL

1. The Disciple's Fast: To Break Sin's Addiction
2. The Ezra Fast: To Solve a Problem
3. The Samuel Fast: For Revival and Soulwinning
4. The Elijah Fast: To Break Depression and Discouragement
5. The Widow's Fast: To Minister to the Needy
6. The Saint Paul's Fast: For Wisdom and Decision-Making
7. The Daniel Fast: For Physical Health
8. The John the Baptist Fast: For Spiritual Testimony
9. The Esther Fast: For Spiritual Protection

addiction

> "Is not this the fast that I have chosen? to loose the bands of wickedness, to undo the heavy burdens, and to let the oppressed go free, and that ye break every yoke? Is it not to deal thy bread to the hungry, and that thou bring the poor that are cast out to thy house? When thou seest the naked, that thou cover him; and that thou hide not thyself from thine own flesh? Then shall thy light break forth as the morning, and thine health shall spring forth speedily; and thy righteousness shall go before thee; the glory of the Lord shall be thy rereward (rear guard)." – Isaiah 58:6-8

INTRODUCTION TO FASTING

A. INTRODUCTION
(Taken from the book *Fasting For Spiritual Breakthrough,* by Elmer Towns, Regal Books, Ventura, CA, 1995)

1. Christian fasting is a non-required ___discipline___ that
   a. ___Alters___ your diet, or
   b. ___Eliminates___ food and/or drink
   c. for a ___biblical purpose___,
   d. accompanied with ___prayer___.

2. Richard Foster said there has not been a significant work on fasting in 100 years. Why?
   a. ___Boomers___

b. _Addiction / food_
c. _No revival_
d. _Need discipline and character_
e. Abundance of food has _isolated us from realities of hunger_
f. Not _healthier_
g. No _testimony_
h. Growth of _demonic forces_

B. KINDS OF FASTS

1. _Normal_ fast is going without food for a certain period of time, drinking only liquid (water and/or juice).
2. _Absolute_ fast, no water or food at all. Should be short.
3. _Partial_ fast, omitting certain foods on a schedule of limited eating, i.e., only one meal a day, only vegetables, etc.
4. The _Wesley_ fast is eating only bread (whole grain) and water.
5. _Rotation_ fast is eating or omitting certain families of food for a designated time. One family of food is eaten every day. The Mayo Clinic fast is eating only one food group a day, omitting the other food groups, used as medical research to determine reaction (allergies) to a particular food group.
6. _Supernatural_

C. HOW TO BEGIN FASTING

1. Ask God to _lead_ in your fast. Jesus describes fasting in the context of the Lord's Prayer – Matt. 6:9-15. "When ye fast, be not . . . of a sad countenance . . . but anoint thy head, and wash thy face, that thou appear not unto men to fast." – Matt. 6:16-18
    a. _private_ for a personal request
    b. _Joint_ for a group project

2. Write out your _purpose_, _plan_ and _length_.

3. Begin with a _one day fast_, i.e., the (Yom Kippur) Day of Atonement Fast. "On the tenth day of the seventh month of each year, you must go without eating to show sorrow for your sins." – Lev. 16:29, CEV. The Yom Kippur Fast is from sundown to sundown (Jewish day).

4. _Eat a light snack_ before sundown (English high tea).

5. Dedicate time for meals _to prayer_.

6. Bring Bible, books, notes, etc., (see specific fast).

D. QUESTIONS ABOUT FASTING

1. What fast is best for the first time? _Normal Yom Yippur_
2. What day of the week is best to fast? _Monday_
3. How long can an absolute fast be planned? _Three days_
4. Should I fast if I have a medical problem? _Be careful_
   a. Treat food as medicine
   b. God will never ask us to harm ourselves
   c. Enter the spirit of the fast
5. Can I fast and still go to work? _yes_
6. Can I fast if I have business or personal responsibilities? _Yes_
7. Why should I fast in secret? "That thou appear not unto men to fast, but unto thy Father which is in secret: and thy Father which seeth in secret, shall reward thee openly." – Matt. 6:18
8. Why should I publicize my fast? _Outward goals_
   a. To commit self and others
   b. As a statement of faith
9. What steps should I follow to lead a group in fasting?
   a. Meet together
   b. Reinforce reason to fast
   c. Begin together
10. What can I drink during a normal fast? _Juice (V8, coffee)_
    a. Non-nutrient
    b. Non-enjoyable
    c. The Law of Silence: When God hasn't spoken, don't make rules.
11. Is a 40-day fast possible today? _Ronnie Floyd – Bill Bright_
12. Is fasting legalism? _Can be_
13. Can you fast for more than one prayer request at a time? _Related to purpose_
14. What happens if you violate your fast? _Begin again_
15. Can children fast? _Probably not_

E. HISTORY OF FASTING

1. The verb "fast" comes from *tsum*, i.e., self-denial. Began with loss of appetite during times of _distress and emergency_. "Hannah was in great distress about her barrenness, and wept and did not eat." – I Sam. 1:7, ELT
2. Associated with "afflicting one's soul and body." – see II Sam. 3:25, ELT
3. People began fasting to turn away God's _anger and judgment_ –I Kings 21:27
4. Fasting was used to seek divine _favor_.
5. _Jesus_ began His ministry with a 40-day fast.
6. Jesus' apostles were criticized for not fasting by the Pharisees and the disciples of John the Baptist.
7. There is no specific guideline that is _prescribed_ or command to fast. It is a discipline that is voluntary.

8. The New Testament _church leaders_ were fasting and worshipping God. – Acts 13:2. When God moved them to send out missionaries, they did it by fasting and praying. – Acts 13:3

9. The early church fasted on _Wednesday_ and _Friday_ to prevent confusion with Pharisees who fasted on Tuesday and Thursday. "Who does not know that the fast of the fourth and sixth day of the week are observed by Christians throughout the world" (Epiphanius, Bishop of Salomis, A.D. 315).

10. The early church practiced a series of one-day fasts per week for several weeks before _Easter_. Also the post-apostolic church required a fast before baptism and ordination.

11. England fasted in 1582 for Drake's victory over the Spanish Armada.

12. Jonathan Edwards fasted before preaching, "Sinners in the Hands of an Angry God."

13. Layman's Prayer Revival, 1859.

14. The Pilgrims fasted the day before disembarking the Mayflower.

General Checklist

Purpose: _____

Fast: What you will withhold _____

Begin: Date _____ Time _____

End: Date _____ Time _____

Vow: I believe God is the only answer to my request and that prayer without fasting is not enough to get an answer to my need. Therefore, by faith I am fasting because I need God to work in this matter.

Bible Basis: My Bible promise _____

_____

Resources: What I need during this fast _____

_____

God being my strength and grace being my basis, I commit myself to the above fast.

_____

    Signed   Date

THE DISCIPLE'S FAST
Breaking Sin's Addiction

A. THE PROBLEM OF A BESETTING SIN

1. Many Christians only have a head knowledge that Christ will give them a "way of escape" – I Cor. 10:13, but are in bondage to sin. "Is not this the fast that I have chosen . . . to loose the bonds of wickedness?" – Isa. 58:6

2. Many Christians are ___helpless victims___ to a "besetting sin"
   – Heb. 12:1, an act / attitude that has them in bondage.

3. Many Christians believe ___Satan's lies___. "Your father the Devil . . .
   he is a liar." – John 8:44. They believe:
   a. I tried before and can't ___break it___.
   b. I don't want to but I can't ___help it___.
   c. I need an answer but can't ___find it___.

4. We end up ___lying to ourselves___. We convince ourselves we have
   no power against a sin. "For the good that I would, I do not; but the evil which I
   would not, that I do." – Rom. 7:19

5. Fasting cleanses the body of toxins, poisons, etc.

B. WHEN TO USE THE DISCIPLE'S FAST

1. ___Compulsive behavior or emotional desires___. Some "have a drink,"
   but break drunkenness when they are converted. For others, drink "has them."
   Can be physical addiction or spiritual addiction.
   ___Physical addiction___ or drug addiction.
2. Sexual addiction.
3. Addiction can be to a number of things, people, and activities.

> Whatever controls my mind controls my life.

C. PRESCRIPTION FOR DISCIPLE'S FAST – MATT. 17:14-21

The disciples prayed for the release of a demon-possessed boy, but "they could not"
– Matt. 17:16 – cast out the demon. Jesus delivered the boy. The following are
principles used by the disciples for breaking bondage:

1. First the victim must make a life-freeing ___choice___ to be delivered.
   "Lord have mercy on my son." – Matt. 17:15
2. Recognize an ___external power___ is responsible for bondage.
   "Jesus rebuked the Devil and he departed from him." – Matt. 17:18
3. Confess your previous ___lack of faith___. "Because of your unbelief"
   – Matt. 17:20
4. State your ___faith – purpose___ of the fast. "If ye have faith as a grain of
   mustard seed, ye shall say unto this mountain, remove hence" – Matt. 17:20
5. Fast ___specifically___ for freedom from the besetting sin. "This kind
   goeth not out but by prayer and fasting" – Matt. 17:21
6. Fast ___repeatedly___ until a breakthrough – Matt. 17:21

You don't have the power to obey until you make a choice to obey

> When you take control of your physical appetite by fasting, you develop strength to take control of your emotional appetites.

D. PRESCRIPTION FOR DELIVERANCE

Pray the following six prayers to deal specifically with the causes of your bondage. Using these prescriptions with prayer and fasting can give freedom from sin.

1. You must ___recognize___ any control over your mind and life. "For the weapons of our warfare are not carnal, but mighty through God to the pulling down of strongholds. Casting down imaginations, and every high thing that exalteth itself against the knowledge of God, and bringing into captivity every thought to the obedience of Christ." – II Cor. 10:4,5
   a. Recognize any ungodly or anti-Christian influence in your home or an alien bond on your life.
   b. Recognize any occult, New Age, or other religious influences in your life.
   c. You fast and pray: "I ___recognize___ . . ."

2. You must ___acknowledge___ your self-deception.
   a. Thinking you don't have to do, "deceiving your ownselves." – James 1:22
   b. Thinking you are above sin, "we deceive ourselves." – I John 1:8
   c. Thinking you are something, "deceiveth himself." – Gal. 6:3
   d. Thinking you are smart, "deceive himself." – I Cor. 3:18
   e. Thinking you can get away with sin, "be not deceived." – Gal. 6:9
   f. You fast and pray: "I ___acknowledge___ . . ."

3. You must ___forgive___ others to get freedom from bitterness.
   a. If you refuse, Satan has an advantage. – II Cor. 2:10-11
   b. If you continually bring up the past, you are in bondage to the past.
   c. If you don't want to let them off the hook, it means they have you on the hook.
   d. If you forgive them, you choose to live with the consequences. If you don't, you still live with the consequences.
   e. If you can't forgive, you are in bondage to them. You don't forgive them for their sake; you forgive them for your sake.
   f. The issue must no longer be between you and them, but between you and God.
   g. You must fast and pray: "I ___forgive___ . . ."

4. You must overcome ___rebellion___ in your life.
   a. You are to submit to civil government – Rom. 13:1-7, church leadership – Heb. 13:17, parents – Eph. 6:1-3, husband, wife, – I Peter 3:1-4, employers – I Peter 2:13-23, and God – Dan. 9:5,9.

b. You must fast and pray: "I ____submit____ . . ."

5. You must take ____responsibility____ for sin in your life.
   a. To continually sin, is to be in bondage to that sin.
   b. God will forgive each sin. "If we confess our sins, He is faithful and just to forgive . . . and cleanse . . ." – I John 1:9
   c. You must fast and pray: "I ~~renounce~~ am responsible . . ."

6. You must ____renounce____ sinful influences from family and friends.
   a. Be aware of the predisposition to sin because of immoral atmosphere, wrong heroes, suggestions by others, desire to please others, or genetics.
   b. You must fast and pray: "I ____renounce____ . . ."

E. PRINCIPLES TO TAKE AWAY

1. The ____purpose____ principle. You may have to fast many times.
2. The ____prescription____ principle. You may have to fast for a long time.
3. The ____inner journey____ principle.
4. The ____daily____ principle. You must repent completely and you must repent daily, i.e., Alcoholic Anonymous.
5. The ____focus____ principle. We fast to break a specific sin.
6. The ____prescription____ principle. When we fast, we should learn to pray the exact words that deal with our bondage.
7. The ____truth - encounter____ principle. We never gain an outward victory over sin until we take inner responsibility for our attitude and actions.

> A person cannot journey without, until he journeys within.

THE EZRA FAST
To Solve a Problem

A. INTRODUCTION

The Ezra Fast is to solve problems in your life that are serious. These are not the everyday types of problems. These involve selling a house, hiring an important person, obtaining money, etc. "Is not this the fast that I have chosen . . . to undo the heavy burdens." – Isa. 58:6

1. Everyone ____has problems____. "Man that is born of woman is of few days, and full of trouble." – Job 14:1. "Yet man is born into trouble as surely as the sparks fly upward." – Job 5:7, NIV

2. Wrong view of problems.
   a. You are ____unsaved____

b. You are ___unspiritual___

c. God has forsaken you.

3. Three questions you ask about your problems:

> **WHY ME?**
> **WHY NOW?**
> **WHY THIS?**

4. Life is like a game. "He who makes the fewest errors . . . wins."
   a. ___Can not run from problems.___
   b. ___Can not stop problems.___
   c. ___You can solve them.___

B. KNOW THE SIX STEPS TO PROBLEM SOLVING

> **HOW TO SOLVE PROBLEMS**
> 1. Get ___facts___
> 2. Establish needed biblical principles.
> 3. ___Write out___ the problem, i.e., clarify it.
> 4. Make a list of ___various ways___ to solve the problem.
> 5. Choose the best solution.
> 6. Implement the solution the ___best way possible___.

C. ISRAEL FACED A PROBLEM – EZRA 8:21-23

The Jews had to return from captivity back to their land. Ezra was the leader to lead the Israelites to return.

1. The ___problem protection___. They needed protection in their march across the wilderness. "I was ashamed to require of the king a band of soldiers . . . to help us against the enemy in the way." – Ezra 8:22

2. On the ___spot___. "Because we had spoken unto the king, saying, the hand of our God is upon all them for good that seek Him." – Ezra 8:22

3. They had to transport lots of ___money___. "In all there were: 25 tons of silver; 100 silver articles weighing 150 pounds; . . . 7,500 pounds of gold." – Ezra 8:25, CEV

4. Fasted about the ___problem___. "So we fasted and asked God Himself to protect us, and He answered our prayer." – Ezra 8:23, ELT

D. PRESCRIPTION FOR THE EZRA FAST

1. Get those involved to fast ___with you___. "I proclaimed a fast." – Ezra 8:21

2. ___Share___ the problem. "We humbled ourselves and asked God to bring us and our children safely to Jerusalem." – Ezra 8:21, CEV

3. Fast _seriously_ to God. "That we might afflict ourselves before our God." – Ezra 8:21

4. Fast _before attempting_ a solution. "I gathered them together to the river that runneth to Ahava and there we abode in tents three days." – Ezra 8:15

5. Fast _on sight with insight_. "Beside the Ahava River I asked the people to go without eating and to pray." – Ezra 8:21, CEV

6. Fast for _step-by-step_ guidance. There were several roads to Jerusalem "to seek of Him a right road" – Ezra 8:21, ELT. "We draw our map to the destination, but God directs each step on the road." – Prov. 16:1, ELT

7. Take _practical steps_ as well as fast to solve the problem. "So we went without food and asked God to protect us." – Ezra 8:23, CEV. Ezra realized some parts of his caravan might be lost. "Then I weighed the gifts . . . I divided them among the twelve priests." – Ezra 8:24, ELT

    a. He divided up the money so all wouldn't be lost.
    b. He made each accountable by weighing it first.

E. PRACTICAL STEPS TOWARD PROBLEM SOLVING

1. Three causes of problems are:
    a. _Change_
    b. Differences in people
    c. Circumstances

2. Three questions to ask:
    a. How _big_ is the problem?
    b. _who_ is involved in the problem?
    c. What do others think about the problem?

3. Three attitudes toward the problem:
    a. _Fuss_
    b. _Fight_
    c. _Die ("I will quit")_

4. Five problem-solving eyes:
    a. Eyes to see the _positive_.
    b. Eyes to see the _people_ involved,
    c. Eyes to see the _facts_.
    d. Emotional eyes blinded with _tears_.
    e. Fearful eyes blinded with _terror_.

> When you don't have facts, the problem grows, you lose perspective, you surrender your values, you blame others or yourself.

5. The bigger the problem . . . the longer your fast . . . or the more often you fast . . . or the more people who fast with you.

6. Bring resources to the Ezra Fast, i.e., personal records, bills, etc.

THE SAMUEL FAST
For Revival and Soul Winning

A. INTRODUCTION

"Is not this the fast that I have chosen . . . to let the oppressed go free?" – Isa. 58:6

1. We are to fast for evangelism or revival.
2. Definition of revival: "God . . . pouring Himself on His people." Revival verse: "Time of refreshing shall come from the presence of the Lord." – Acts 3:10, ELT

B. PRESCRIPTION FOR THE SAMUEL FAST

The Samuel Fast has a threefold action, i.e., pre-fast preparation, and the actual fast and post-fast action.

Pre-Fast Preparation

1. Recognition of your _____. Some are in bondage to habits, sins, others, demons, the past, etc. "Don't stop praying!" They told Samuel, "Ask the Lord our God to rescue us." – I Sam. 7:8, CEV. "The Lord (had) delivered them into the hands of the Philistines." – Judges 13:1
2. Renew allegiance to _____ among His people. Today, the presence of God is in His church. "The church, which is His body." – Eph. 1:22-23. To prepare for revival, the people:
   a. Recognized the need for God's presence among them. "The men . . . fetched up the ark of the Lord." – I Sam. 7:1
   b. Assembled the people at God's place. "Gather all Israel to Mizpah." – I Sam. 7:5
3. Type of fast for revival and/or evangelism.
   a. Congregational fast, one day
   b. Weekly fast
   c. 40-hour fast (see book, *Fasting Can Change Your Life.*
   d. 40-day congregational fast with various levels of entry
   e. Leadership fast
   f. Pray and fast during sermon, i.e., watchers
   g. Prayer and fasting clock

During the Actual Fast

4. There must be a _____.
   a. Individual fasting makes a person individually responsible to God. "When ye fast . . . fast unto my Father." – Matt. 6:18, ELT
   b. Corporate fasting makes a person responsible for what God does to the corporate body. "Gather all Israel." – I Sam. 7:5

5. God's people must demonstrate _____. "Israel lamented after the Lord." – I Sam. 7:2. "If ye do return unto the Lord with all your hearts, then put away the strange gods and Ashtaroth from among you." – I Sam. 7:3

6. God's people must _____ and separate from it. "Then the children of Israel did put away Baalim and Ashtaroth." – I Sam. 7:4
   a. Backsliders are _____ to sin in their life.
   b. Backsliders are _____ about sin in their life.
   c. During fasting, God will show hidden sin to the believer, i.e., and the sin that is prohibiting God's blessing.
   d. Fasting must be an ongoing process, and God will gradually reveal sin as we continue to fast.

7. Corporate _____ of sin. The leaders must confess for the group as Daniel privately confessed Israel's corporate sin. "We have sinned." – Dan. 9:5. Each individual must privately confess group sin. "We have sinned against the Lord." – I Sam. 7:6. There is power when a group corporately deals with its sin.

8. God loves _____. The fast is an outer symbol of inner desire for God.
   a. Not eating. "On that same day, they went without eating to show their sorrow, and they confessed they had been unfaithful to the Lord." – I Sam. 7:6a, CEV
   b. Sacrifice to God. "They drew water from the well and poured it out as an offering to the Lord." – I Sam 7:6b, CEV

Post-Fast Actions

9. Post-fasting _____. God may begin to give a victory, but the enemy may counter attack. "The Philistine rulers found out about the meeting at Mizpah. They sent an army there to attack the people of Israel." – I Sam. 7:7, CEV

10. Need for a _____ of fasting and prayer, not just a _____. After they fasted, "The men of Israel were afraid when they heard that the Philistines were coming. "Don't stop praying!" They told Samuel, "Ask the Lord our God to rescue us." – I Sam. 7:7, ELT

11. Need for _____ to follow fasting. "Samuel begged the Lord to rescue Israel, then he sacrificed a young lamb to the Lord. Samuel had not even finished offering the sacrifice when the Philistines started to attack." – I Sam. 7:10a, CEV

12. Look for _____. "The Lord answered his prayer and made thunder crash all around them (enemy). The Philistines panicked and ran away." – I Sam. 7:10b, CEV

13. Victory is a _____, not just a _____. "The Philistines were so badly beaten, that it was quite a while before they attacked Israel again." – I Sam. 7:12, CEV

14. Celebrate with _____. "Samuel took a stone, and set it between Mizpah and Shen, and called the name of it Ebenezer, saying, 'Hitherto hath the Lord helped us.'" – I Sam. 7:12, ELT
   a. Your victory stone should look to the *past* "hath . . . helped us."

b. Your victory stone should look to the *present*, "Ebenezer" which means "Help Stone."

c. Your victory stone should look to the victory, "Hitherto," implying the need of God's help in the *future*.

C. PRINCIPLES TO TAKE AWAY

1. The need for _____ to secure the blessing of God. Israel had been in bondage for years before Samuel came on the scene.

2. The need for _____ among God's people. The people had to "trust and obey" by gathering together, confessing, fasting and seeking God's victory.

3. The need for _____. Some travel to the extreme of only praying for revival. Others travel to the opposite extreme, they think God's blessing comes with programs, meetings, or human activity. "We are co-laborers with God." – I Cor. 3:9, ELT

4. The role of _____ in God's work. A symbol is an outer evidence of an inner reality. We need to demonstrate our inner loyalty to God with outer actions and victory stones.

THE ELIJAH FAST
To Break Depression or Discouragement.

A. INTRODUCTION

1. God promises that fasting can break habits. "Is not this the fast that I have chosen . . . that ye break every yoke." – Isa. 58:6

2. Elijah was used of God, but after a great victory he got depressed and discouraged.

3. The Elijah Fast is to change people's thinking. If their thinking is changed, their actions can be changed. If their actions are changed, their life can be changed.

B. ELIJAH'S HABIT/PROBLEM

Elijah was the bold prophet who stood alone on Mt. Carmel to challenge 450 prophets of Baal. Elijah challenged, "If the Lord be God, follow Him: if Baal, then follow him" – I Kings 18:21. He put God on the spot, "Lord God of Abraham . . . let it be known . . . that I am thy servant, and that I have done all these things at Thy Word" – I Kings 18:36. After victory, Jezebel threatened to kill Elijah, so he ran away. "He went for his life" – I Kings 19:3. Elijah's continuing problem was (1) _____ from people and problems, (2) _____ and/or depression. "He requested for himself that he might die" – I Kings 19:4. And (3) _____. The issue, "How would God break the cycle of pessimistic despondency?"

1. Depression follows _____. "The hand of the Lord was on Elijah." – I Sam. 18:46. Yet after the victory he prayed, "O Lord, take away my life." – I Kings 19:4. Was his boldness a cover-up for pessimistic withdrawal? Was his despondency a reoccurring phenomenon that only appeared at times?

2. God can separate what you mean from _____. Elijah was bold, "I will surely shew myself unto him (King Ahab) today" – I Kings 18:15. "Jezebel sent a messenger unto Elijah . . . if I make not (I will make) thy life as the life of one of them (her killed prophets) by tomorrow" – I Kings 19:2. Yet in fear, he ran away.

3. _____. God worked through Elijah, yet he thought no one else served God. "I only am left." – I Kings 19:2, ELT

4. Past blessings do not prevent _____. "They seek my life to take it away." – I Kings 19:10

C. THE PRESCRIPTION OF THE ELIJAH FAST

1. _____. "He laid down and slept" – I Kings 19:5, ELT. "There was a cake . . . he did eat and drink" – I Kings 19:6. Preparation is physical, mental and emotional.

2. _____. "The journey is too great for thee." – I Kings 19:7.
   a. Admit you cannot do it alone.
   b. Let others help you.

3. _____. "Went in the strength of that meat forty days and forty nights unto Horeb, the Mount of God." – I Kings 19:8
   a. Revisit it _____. This means going back to a location of past spiritual victories.
   b. Revisit _____ by memory and recommitment, i.e., go back to revive a former work of God in your life.
   c. There are places where both God and demons want to _____. Elijah left the land of idols (demon inspired) to return to Sinai (peak), Horeb (range), where God called Moses and gave the Ten Commandments.

4. _____. "The Word of the Lord came to him." – I Kings 19:9
   a. Study to know what God said; not what you think it says. Depressed people believe the credibility of their memory. They need to look outside themselves to see what God says.
   b. Depressed people need a positive message from outside their thinking to break their thought patterns.

5. God knows our _____. "He (God) said unto him, 'What doest thou here, Elijah?'" – I Kings 19:9. Questions are mirrors to make us view ourselves from outside our inner compulsivness.

6. _____. Elijah expressed his depression. "I have been very jealous for the Lord God . . . for the children of Israel have forsaken thy covenant." – I Kings 19:10

7. Search for answers _____.
   People who want to break a habit usually ask God to do it for them or to give them an external power to overcome it. Habits are broken the way they are formed . . . gradually . . . one act at a time . . . by submitting . . . by repetition.

> "Behold the Lord passed by, and a great and strong wind rent the mountains, and brake in pieces the rocks . . . but the Lord was not in the wind: and after the wind an earthquake, but the Lord was not in the earthquake: and after the earthquake, a fire, but the Lord was not in the fire: and after the fire, a still small voice." – I Kings 19:11-12

8. Look at the problem through _____. Don't focus negatively on breaking habits but on "seeing" the positive. God told Elijah, "I have left me seven thousand in Israel all the knees which have not bowed unto Baal." – I Kings 19:18
9. Habits are broken by following _____, rather than zeroing in on negative traits. Notice God does not tell Elijah to "quit being depressed" or to "stop grumbling." God gave the depressed prophet some positive actions. "Go . . . anoint Hazael." – I Kings 19:15. "Jehu . . . shalt thou anoint." – I Kings 19:16. "Go and anoint . . . Elisha." – I Kings 19:16
   a. Don't focus only on breaking a wrong habit.
   b. Focus on positive actions that will establish good habits.

YOU CAN'T ACHIEVE
WHAT YOU CAN'T CONCEIVE

10. People break bad habits when they perceive themselves doing _____.
    God instructed Elijah, "Go . . . anoint . . . Elisha . . . to be prophet in thy room."
    – I Kings 19:16

D. PRINCIPLES TO TAKE AWAY

1. When you know what forms good character you know how to break bad habits.
2. Focus on the biblical principles of strength and separation in fasting and prayer.
3. Fast and pray for God to give you a foundation of biblical character. "Character is habitually doing the right thing, in the right way."
4. Fast and pray for the positive actions God would have you do.
5. Develop a list of prayer requests for times of fasting and watch your confidence grow as you record answers to your prayers.

BUILDING CHARACTER

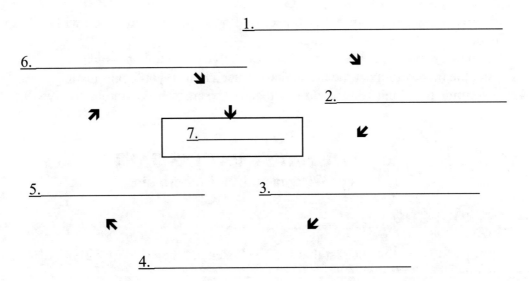

1. _____

6. _____

2. _____

7. _____

5. _____   3. _____

4. _____

THE WIDOW'S FAST
To Minister to the Needy

PROBLEM

The Widow's Fast involves giving up your food to meet the need of others, especially their humanitarian needs such as food, clothing, and shelter. It is called the Widow's Fast because widows gave up all to help the needs of others. – I Kings 17:11-15

KEY VERSE

"Is it not to share your bread with the hungry, and that you bring to your house the poor who are cast out; when you see the naked that you cover him, and not hide yourself from your own flesh?" – Isa. 58:7

PRESCRIPTION

1. Become others-oriented by being sensitive to the problems experienced by those you come in contact with or hear about.
2. Recognize how much better off you are than others appear to be.
3. Give to help meet the need from resources that you would consume on yourself.
4. Ask for wisdom to determine the extent to which you should be involved in a humanitarian project.
5. Pray for wisdom during your fast.
6. Attempt to identify with their suffering during your fast.
7. Consider making a permanent life-style change that would enable you to continue contributing to the humanitarian needs of others.

PRACTICAL

1. Identify the specific humanitarian need and/or project in which you will become involved.
2. Estimate amount of goods you would normally consume in a typical day.
3. Send the money to meet the humanitarian need before you begin fasting.
4. Determine how long you should fast to save the amount you intend to give this project.

THE SAINT PAUL'S FAST
For Wisdom and Decision-Making

A. INTRODUCTION

1. Promise: "Is not this the fast that I have chosen . . . then shall thy light break forth as the morning?" – Isa. 58:6,8
2. Christians need help facing the many major decisions they face in their private, spiritual, business, family, and church life. The Saint Paul Fast is designed for major decisions, not the everyday decisions of life.

B. PRE-FAST PREPARATION

Before you begin to fast about a decision, you need to have a strategy of decision-making. Begin by knowing how to make decisions and having information you need to make a decision.

STEPS IN DECISION-MAKING

1. Honestly _face your decisions_ .
   a. Know you have a problem
   b. Know you must do something
   c. Know you can solve it
2. _Define_ your problem.
   a. Don't work on symptoms
   b. Write out the problem (a well-defined problem is half solved)
3. Gather _information_ .
   a. Write out facts about your problem
   b. Look at causes
   c. Evaluate assumptions
4. Develop as many alternate solutions as possible. Evaluate each alternative. (It is important to write out as many solutions to your problem as come to your mind).
5. Choose the _best decision_ .
   a. To make a decision without the above process is guessing
   ⓑ Decision-making is not thinking up what to do, it is choosing the best solution suggested
   c. In an imperfect world, there is no perfect answer only the best solution at this time
6. Make the decision _work_ .
   a. Communication to those involved
   b. Constant evaluation
   c. Check your goal

C. PRESCRIPTION FOR THE ST. PAUL'S FAST

Paul had the wrong idea about Christianity and the wrong idea about God. He was going in the wrong way, doing the wrong thing, with the wrong attitude. How can one so wrong be turned around?

1. Set aside a fasting time so you can listen for the _voice of Jesus_ . Saul "fell to the earth and heard a voice." – Acts 9:4. "He was three days . . . neither did eat or drink." – Acts 9:9. "Be still and know that I am God." – Psa. 46:10
2. Ask and answer searching questions _about yourself_ .
   a. God asked Saul, "Why persecutest thou me?" – Acts 9:4. Sometimes we think we're on God's side, but "He that is not for me, is against me." When God comes looking for us, He uses a question to make us think. "Adam, where art thou?" "Cain why are you mad?"
   b. Saul asked God, "Who art thou Lord?" – Acts 9:5. Until we want to know God, He will not show Himself to us.

3. Recognize the unchangeable _Solitude of truth_. The answer may be silently waiting for us to find it. When we fast, we search for it. But we deceive ourselves when we try to justify ourselves, make things go our way, thinking we are never wrong.
   a. Realize answers are outside yourself. Saul, "trembling and astonished." – Acts 9:6
   b. Look to Heaven as Saul said, "Lord." – Acts 9:6
4. You must stop all self-effort and _yield to God_. There is a time for self-effort to take responsibility for your problems. But you are fasting because you need help and wisdom for a decision/problem.
   a. Your outer reflects the inner. Paul, "fell to the earth." – Acts 9:4. "And he trembling and astonished said, 'Lord, what wilt thou have me to do?'" – Acts 9:6
   b. He was admitting his past mistakes and yielding his prejudices.
5. The St. Paul's Fast is _searching_ for answers/wisdom. Saul asked, "Lord, what wilt thou have me to do?" – Acts 9:6
   a. We actively search. "Ye shall find Me, when ye search for Me with all your heart." – Jer. 29:13
   b. Allow the Lord to search us. "I the Lord, search the heart." – Jer. 17:10
   c. The Holy Spirit teaches, "The Comforter, which is the Holy Spirit, He shall teach you all things, and bring all things to your remembrance, whatsoever I have said to you." – John 14:26, ELT
   d. Your task – "Study to shew thyself approved unto God, a workman that needeth not to be ashamed, rightly dividing the Word of Truth." – II Tim. 2:15
   e. Your prayer – "Search me O God, and know my heart; try me, and know my thoughts . . . and lead me in the way everlasting." – Psalm 139:23-24
6. Write down what you learn from God – "The Lord said unto him (Saul), Arise and go into the city" – Acts 9:6. "And Saul arose . . . (they) brought him into Damascus" – Acts 9:8. "I was not disobedient unto the heavenly vision." – Acts 26:19
7. Your answer may be an _embryonic seed._, not a full-grown tree. Saul was not given all the solutions/answers to his problem. God told him, "Arise, and go into the city, and it shall be told thee what thou must do." – Acts 9:6
   a. You may have to fast longer or more than once for the answer. "He was three days without sight, and neither did eat nor drink." – Acts 9:9
   b. Praying and fasting may bring light like the gradual dawning of a new day.
8. God may use _others_ to give you insight/wisdom. "Ananias . . . entered into the house, and putting his hands on him said, Brother Saul, the Lord, even Jesus . . . hath sent me, that thou mightest receive thy sight and be filled with the Holy Ghost." – Acts 9:17
9. People may not _understand_ your St. Paul's Fast or what God is doing in your life. "The men which journeyed with him stood speechless, hearing a voice, but seeing no man." – Acts 9:7
   a. They didn't see Jesus.
   b. They weren't asked, nor did they fast.
   c. They didn't get God's answer from Ananias.

D. PRINCIPLES TO TAKE AWAY

1. The more __*weight*__ your decision, the more often or longer you should follow the St. Paul's Fast.
2. Plan Bible reading that is not directly related to your decision so your mind can relax in God's presence. You may find your answer in the quietness of peace. Some try to read the New Testament in one day.
3. Get all __*information*__ and bring it to the St. Paul's Fast. Bring charts, reports, etc. to the St. Paul's Fast.
4. Know and apply principles of decision-making.
5. Write out the __*decision*__ you need to make during the St. Paul's Fast.
6. Write out __*facts*__ that influenced your decision and review them with prayer.
7. Write out all __*possible solutions*__ before attempting to make a decision.
8. Now you are ready to ask God to help you with an answer/solution.

THE DANIEL FAST
For Physical Health

A. INTRODUCTION

1. Fasting is one discipline that will heal/improve health. "Is not this the fast that I have chosen . . . and thy health shall spring forth speedily?" – Isa. 58:8, ELT
2. God __*heals*__, *Jehovah Rapha*. "I am the Lord that healeth thee." – Ex. 15:26
3. Healing comes by __*faith*__ and prayer. "The prayer of faith shall save the sick, and the Lord shall raise him up." – James 5:15
4. The body __*heals itself*__. Doctors, surgical procedures, and medicine only remove the cause of disease/ill health.
5. Correct diet will make you __*healthier*__. You are what you eat, i.e., if you put good food into your body, you will have a healthy body. When you put the wrong/unhealthy food into your body, you will be sick or unhealthy.

B. THE DANIEL FAST PRESCRIPTION

1. Begin your fast by defining __*the problem*__, then pray for a specific answer to that problem. Daniel faced the problem (wrong diet) and the prospect (poor health). Why did Daniel reject the king's diet? "The king appointed them a daily provision of the king's meat, and the wine which he drank." – Dan. 1:15, ELT
   a. Against Jewish __*dietary laws*__
   b. Alcoholic, i.e., __*prohibited*__
   c. Offered to foreign __*gods / demons*__
2. Fast as a __*spiritual commitment*__ to God for His answer. "Daniel purposed in his heart that he would not defile himself." – Daniel 1:8. A spiritual commitment is first and greater than any dietary commitment.

3. Your _fast commitment_ is an outer test that reflects an inner desire. "Please test your servants for ten days: Give them nothing but vegetables to eat and water to drink" – Daniel 1:12, NIV. The physical health you seek may be tied to several factors:
   a. Your _dietary_ commitment is reflected in your choice of certain food and the prohibition of others.
   b. Your _spiritual_ commitment is reflected in constant prayer during the fast.
   c. Your _time_ commitment is reflective by carrying your fast to its natural conclusion.
   d. Your _testimony_ commitment is reflective of your faith. You have told others that you are fasting for a specific purpose. "If ye have faith . . . ye shall say unto this mountain (your physical problem), remove hence . . ." – Matt. 17:20. Therefore the answer may be tied to completion of your fast/diet.
   e. When _breaking_ your fast, you reject your spiritual commitment.
4. Fast and pray to understand the _role of sin_ that keeps you from health/healing. "Now Daniel resolved not to defile himself . . . he asketh the chief official for permission not to defile himself in this way." – Daniel 1:8, NIV

→ physical.

> "Is any sick among you? Let him call for the elders of the church: and let them pray over him, anointing him with oil in the name of the Lord: And the prayer of faith shall save the sick, and the Lord shall raise him up; and if he have committed sins, they shall be forgiven him." – James 5:14-16

   a. Sin sometimes is related to a person's lack of health/healing.
   b. Your lack of health/healing may be tied to spiritual rebellion, i.e., adultery, lying, blasphemy, etc. It could also be the sin of wrong intake, i.e., alcohol, drugs, cigarettes, etc. It could be a poor diet, i.e., fatty foods, poisonous foods, etc.
5. Your fast is a statement of faith _to others_. Definition: "Faith is affirming what God said in His Word." Daniel said, "Give us nothing but vegetables to eat . . . then compare our appearance with the young men who eat the royal food." – Dan. 1:13, NIV.
6. The Daniel Fast is not done _privately_. The Daniel Fast is a statement of faith. "The official told Daniel, I am afraid of my lord the king . . . why should he see you looking worse?" – Dan. 1:10, NIV. "Daniel then said to the guard . . . please test thy servants for ten days." – Dan. 1:11-12, ELT
   a. More than one can agree to fast together
   b. Announce to others the purpose of the fast
   c. Relate your sin to those involved
   d. Involve church leaders in your fast

there's vd   , is

there is value in the volume of prayer. God will stop the progress of the disease. but won't restore destroyed members.

Spiritual Foundations of Church Growth   66   Dr. Elmer L. Towns
Chapter Nine

7. Know the _____potential_____ of the food you eat during the Daniel Fast. "So the guard took away their choice of food and the wine . . . and gave them vegetables instead." – Dan. 1:16, NIV. Daniel lived to be over 90 years old.

8. Yield all ___physical results___ to God. Daniel submitted himself to the consequences of his convictions. "As thou seest, deal with thy servants." – Daniel 1:13
   a. Did Daniel say, "I won't eat it, so you will have to punish/kill me?"
   b. Did Daniel say, "If my diet doesn't make me better, I'll eat your diet?"
   c. Did Daniel say, "My diet will make me better, then you will decide to leave us on this diet?"

9. It may not be God's will to heal you because of your fasting and prayer.
   a. The disease has ___endangered___ other physical organs/functions.
   b. You began fasting and prayer ___too late___, i.e.; you previously disobeyed and didn't begin when God spoke to you.
   c. You did not repent ___deep enough___.
   d. Your sickness is God's punishment for a ___sin / rebellion___.

10. The Daniel Fast will lead to ___spiritual insight___. "To these four young men, God gave knowledge and understanding." – Dan. 1:17, NIV. "The king talked to them and he found none equal to (those who fast)" – Dan. 1:19, NIV. "In every matter of wisdom and understanding about which the king questioned them, he found them ten times better than all." – Dan. 1:20, NIV

C. PRACTICAL TO TAKE AWAY

1. The Daniel Fast is longer than ___one day___, because your health/sickness is developed over a long time.

2. The Daniel Fast is a ___partial___ fast. It does not mean to take away all food and water.

3. The Daniel Fast involves ___healthy___ food. Inasmuch as "the body heals itself," you must allow basic necessities to strengthen the body so it can heal itself.

4. The Daniel Fast involves ___abstinence___ from "party" food. While there may be times to enjoy "party" food, the Daniel Fast is a return to basic necessities.

THE JOHN THE BAPTIST FAST
For Spiritual Testimony

A. INTRODUCTION

1. The John the Baptist Fast is to establish your influence and testimony for the glory of God in an evil world. "Is not this the fast that I have chosen . . . and thy righteousness shall go before thee?" – Isa. 58:6,8. The John the Baptist Fast is both a one-time fast and an ongoing fast.

2. You can fast for your testimony to certain persons, at certain locations or in the face of problems.

3. You can fast for the testimony of your pastor, church or Christian organization.

B. ESTABLISHING A GREAT TESTIMONY

1. _____. "Among them that are born of women there hath not risen a greater than John the Baptist." – Matt. 11:11.
2. Diet _____. "He shall be great in the sight of the Lord, and shall drink neither wine nor strong drink." – Luke 1:15. His Nazarite vow made him different from average people.
3. _____. "He (John) will be filled with the Holy Spirit, even from his birth." –Lev. 1:15, NIV
4. Evangelistic _____. "Many of the people of Israel will he bring back to the Lord their God." – Lev. 1:16, NIV
5. Influence _____. "He will go . . . in the spirit and power of Elijah, to turn the hearts of the fathers to their children, and the disobedient to the wisdom of the righteous to make ready a people for the Lord." – Luke 1:14, NIV
6. _____. "(None) greater than John the Baptist, not withstanding, he that is least in the kingdom of heaven is greater than he." – Matt. 11:11

C. PRESCRIPTION FOR THE JOHN THE BAPTIST FAST

1. Attach your special diet/fast to your _____. "He will be great in the sight of the Lord. He is never to take wine or other fermented drink." – Lev. 1:15, NIV
2. _____ the areas where you want influence. "There was a man sent from God whose name was John . . . came for a witness to bear witness of the Light." – John 1:6-7. What are you sent for?
3. Your fast/diet makes you a _____. John the Baptist was dedicated as a Nazarite from birth. Nazarite comes from *Nadhar* "to vow," hence a Nazarite is "a person of the vow," i.e., dedicated or consecrated to God as evidence by food and clothes that set him apart. Nazarite vows were temporary (usually 30 days) or permanent (from birth), and were usually instituted by distress or trouble.
4. Recognize you become influential by _____. To be an influence, repent and bring your total life into conformity to Christ.
   a. _____. "John's clothes were made of camel's hair" – Matt. 3:4, NIV – not camel skin, but cloth woven with hair, i.e., peasant's clothes.
   b. _____. "His fast was locust and wild honey." – Matt. 3:4, ELT. Locust was "clean" food to the Jewish dietary law. – Lev. 11:22
   c. No _____. "He is never to take wine or other fermented drink." – Num. 6:3, ELT
   d. _____.
5. The John the Baptist Fast is _____ and _____. Whereas some fasts are a crisis event (the Apostle's Fast) and some fasts are lengthy (the Daniel Fast), this fast is both because our testimony is involved with crises and ongoing influences.

6. Long-term (because of long-term problems) as reflected in a long-term _____. The act of separating oneself for spiritual purposes is a life-long practice. However, during the John the Baptist Fast:
    a. Write out your commitment
    b. Determine its length
    c. Write out the purpose (the more exact your aim, the better you can attack an unanswered prayer)
    d. Make a vow and sign it
7. Short-term fast for immediate issues. These are issues that distress us.

D. PRACTICAL TO TAKE AWAY

1. Determine _____ for the short and long-range fast/diet. Make these a matter of prayer and write the duration before you begin a fast/diet.
2. Determine _____ before you begin. These should be written down before beginning the fast. Ask yourself:
    a. Is this healthy for me?
    b. Will this harm me?
    c. Would this be a testimony if others knew what I was doing?
    d. Is this mere legalism? (trying to please God by the flesh).
    e. Why am I withdrawing from this food/liquid?
3. Determine _____ before you begin. "He (Jesus) who is coming after me is preferred before me, whose shoe's latchet I am not worthy to unloose." – John 1:27

THE ESTHER FAST
For spiritual protection

A. INTRODUCTION

The Esther Fast is used to protect you from the attacks of demons and Satan directly, and from secondary things they will use against you.

1. "Is not this the fast that I have chosen . . . the glory of the Lord shall be thy reward?" – Isa. 58:6,8
2. Protected by _____. "The Lord went before them by day in a pillar of a cloud (Shekinah) . . . and by night in a pillar of fire, to give them light to go by day and night." – Ex. 13:21. "And the pillar of the cloud went from before their face, and stood behind them." – Ex. 14:19
3. Life is a _____ between competitive forces. "We wrestle not against flesh and blood, but against principalities, against powers, against the rulers of the darkness of this world, against wickedness in high places." – Eph. 6:12
4. When Satan gets to us, he gets to _____. "The people you forgave for sinning against your church, I forgive, because Satan gets to us if we have an

unforgiving spirit. I forgive them because I live in Christ. I am not ignorant of Satan's devices to get to me." – II Cor. 2:10-11, ELT

B. THE PROBLEM – ESTHER 3:1-4:17

Haman hated the Jews because they would not bow down to him – 3:3. He used his position to pass a law to allow the Persians to eliminate the Jews. People/Satan hate Christians because they will not bow (compromise) to ungodly principles. Queen Esther was told she couldn't hide her Jewish ancestry in the palace. She had to get involved but she could possibly lose her life if she tried.

C. THE PRESCRIPTION FOR THE ESTHER FAST

1. Recognize _____ of danger and destruction. "Mordecai gave a copy . . . of the decree . . . to destroy them . . . to shew it to Esther." – 4:8
2. Realize you are under demonic _____. We have an enemy. "Your adversary the devil, as a roaring lion, walketh about, seeking whom he may devour." – I Peter 5:8
3. Recognize what _____ protects you. Mordecai told Esther, "She should go into the king to make requests before him for her people." – 4:8. Principles of fighting satanic influence:
   a. _____. "Flee these things." – I Tim. 6:11
   b. _____. "Resist the devil, and he will flee from you." – James 4:7. "Fight the good fight of faith." – I Tim. 6:12
   c. _____. You cannot rebuke the devil in your power but in God's power. "Michael the Archangel when contending with the devil . . . for the body of Moses, dared not bring against him a railing accusation, but said, 'the Lord rebuke thee.'" – Jude 9
4. Fast and pray for _____. Esther instructed Mordecai, "I also and my maidens will fast likewise." – 4:16. The seventh petition of the Lord's prayer. "Deliver us from the Evil One." – Matt. 6:13, NKJV
5. Know the _____ of prayer and fasting. There are some things fasting will not do for you. "I will go into the king which is not according to the law: and if I perish." – 4:16
   a. Fasting did not change the decree.
   b. Fasting did not make the king call the queen.
   c. Fasting did not solve the crisis.
   d. God has shut Himself up to the circumstances of life and works through them to accomplish His glory and His purpose. God does not violate the free will of people, nor does He violate the nature of His laws.
6. Get power in _____ fasting and prayer. Esther instructed, "Go, gather together all the Jews . . . and fast ye for me, and neither eat or drink three days, night or day, I also and my maidens will fast." – 4:16. Others who called for group fasting for protection:
   a. Samuel faced the Philistines. – I Sam. 8
   b. Joel predicted locusts – Joel 1:14

7. Fast to overcome _____ so you can understand the nature and purpose of spiritual attacks on you. "As the serpent beguiled Eve through his subtlety, so your minds should be corrupted from the simplicity that is in Christ." – II Cor. 11:3
   a. When Satan blinds you, demons don't need to attack you.
   b. When you are successful to overcome satanic blindness, beware of attacks in other realms.
   c. Esther got the king's permission for the Jews to protect themselves, but there was danger and warfare. "That the Jews be ready against that day to avenge themselves on their enemies." – 8:13. "The Jews smote all their enemies." –9:5
8. Fasting must be followed by _____ not reckless abandonment of principles. Note the outward things Esther did to get a solution:
   a. Be in the _____. "Esther stood in the inner court of the king's house." – 5:1
   b. Wear the _____. "Esther put on her royal apparel." – 5:1. Paul warns, "Put on the whole armor of God, that ye may be able to stand against the wiles of the devil." – Eph. 6:11. Hips = Truth. Chest = Righteousness. Feet = Preparation of the Gospel. Defense = Shield of Faith. Head = Helmet of Salvation. Sword = Word of God.
   c. Use _____. Esther invited Haman and the king to a banquet rather than immediately asking her request. Great requests are not blurted out before a king; there must be preparation to build up anticipation.
9. You need _____ against evil spirits. Angels are spirits that God uses in our life. "Are they (angels) not all ministering spirits, sent forth to minister?" –Heb. 1:14. You do not pray to angelic spirits for protection, but many times God uses them to protect His people. – Psa. 34:7, 91:11; Daniel 6:22.

D. PRACTICAL TO TAKE AWAY

1. The greater the _____ on you, the more often you fast, or the longer you fast. It takes more intensity to break a severe attack from Satan. "This kind goeth not out but by prayer and fasting." – Matt. 17:21
2. The greater the spiritual attack on you, the _____ you must get to fast and pray for you.
3. The greater the spiritual attack on you, the _____ you must make for your fast, i.e., time, place, study, tools, etc.
4. While you pray daily for your spiritual protection from the "Evil One" – Matt. 6:13) – you do not fast daily. You fast on a _____ for protection (i.e., once a week, month, etc.).
5. When God puts it upon your heart, fast and pray for the spiritual protection of your spiritual _____.

EPILOGUE: ORGANIZING YOUR CHURCH FOR FASTING

A. WHAT FASTING WILL NOT DO

1. Is not _____. "You humble yourselves by going through the motions . . . is this what you call fasting?" – Isa. 58:5, ELT
2. Will not _____. "What good is fasting when you keep on fighting and quarreling?" – Isa. 58:4, ELT
3. Will not _____. "We have fasted before you, they say. Why aren't you impressed? . . . I will tell you why. It is because you are living for yourself even while you are fasting." – Isa. 58:3, ELT
4. Will not _____. "David therefore besought God for the child: and David fasted . . . neither did he eat bread . . . on the seventh day, the child died" – II Sam. 12:16-18. "While the child was alive, I fasted and wept; for I said, who can tell whether God will be gracious . . . but now he is dead, wherefore should I fast?" – II Sam. 12:22-23

B. THE SPIRITUAL BASIS OF FASTING – JOEL 2:12-32

1. Turn to God with _____. "Turn ye even to me (the Lord) with all your heart, and with fasting and with weeping and with mourning." – Joel 2:12
2. Repent of _____. "Don't tear your clothing, tear your heart." – Joel 2:13, ELT
3. Call a _____. "Declare a fast, call a solemn assembly" – Joel 2:15. A solemn assembly is not for joyful praise, worship, testimony or the preaching of the Word. A solemn assembly is to allow people to search their hearts for sin . . . to confess, to examine motives.
4. Spiritual answers _____. "Then will the Lord be jealous for His land, and pity His people." – Joel 2:18
5. Physical answers _____. "He will cause to come down for you, the former rain, and the latter rain in the first month." – Joel 2:23
6. Spiritual breakthrough and _____. "And I will restore to you the years the locust hath eaten." – Joel 2:25
7. _____. The path to revival is fasting. Revival is defined as "God manifesting. Himself among His people." Joel offers, "I will pour out my spirit upon all flesh." – Joel 2:28
8. _____. Because the people fast and pray, "That whosoever should call upon the name of the Lord shall be (saved) delivered." – Joel 2:32
9. _____. The church that is growing within (spiritual growth) has a foundation for outreach and attendance growth (numerical growth).

C. ACTION STARTERS

1. Would you be willing to become a PRAYER LEADER in your church?
   - ❏ Yes
   - ❏ No
   - ❏ Consider
2. Who could be appointed PRAYER LEADER in your church?

   _____

3. Will you fast one day a month for your church/ministry?
   - ❏ Yes
   - ❏ No
   - ❏ Consider
4. Will you fast once for your church/ministry?
   - ❏ Yes
   - ❏ No

   When?

Let's Get Started

1. Write what you want God to do because of this day studying fasting.

   _____
   _____

2. How long will you fast the first time?
   Begin? _____ End?_____

3. What will you withhold? _____
   _____

4. Who will you ask to join you? _____
   _____

5. What is your prayer promise? _____
   _____

D. JOB DESCRIPTION FOR PRAYER LEADER

1. Gather and print prayer requests.
2. Share requests and needs with leaders.
3. Recruit intercessors.
4. Organize prayer events.
5. Lead prayer meetings.

CHAPTER TEN
MEDITATION

I. INTRODUCTION: THE LOST ART OF MEDITATION

(Taken from the book, *Biblical Meditations for Spiritual Breakthrough*, by Elmer Towns, Regal Books, 1998). This book is available in its entirety online at www.elmertowns.com).

A. _____Command_____. "This book of the law shall not depart out of thy mouth; but thou shalt meditate therein day and night, that thou shalt observe to do according to all that is written therein, for then thou shalt make thy way prosperous, and then thou shalt have good success." – Joshua 1:8

B. Results:
1. So we will __do__ God's will.
2. So we will __prosper/grow__.
3. So we will be __successful/accomplish__.

C. _____Definition_____. "To focus one's thoughts, (ponder), to plan or project in the mind (intend), to engage in contemplation (reflect)" – Webster.

D. Biblical terms to describe meditation:
1. _____Remembering_____
2. _____Think_____ on these things
3. _____Ponder_____
4. _____Beholding_____ God's love
5. Musing on the _____work_____ of God's hands
6. _____Consider_____
7. The _____mind_____ of Christ dwelling in you
8. _____Set your mind_____ on things above
9. Let the _____Word of Christ dwell_____ in you richly

The David Model	Considering God's creation and majesty
The Mary Model	Pondering the person of Jesus
The St. John Model	Thinking about the cross
The Joshua Model	Focusing on biblical principles
The St. Paul Model	Becoming like Christ
The Timothy Model	Meditating on your calling and gifts
The Haggai Model	Considering your failures
The Asaph Model	Meditating on God's intervention
The Malachi Model	Meditating on God's name
The Korah Model	Contemplating Intimacy with God

VIEWS OF MEDITATION

II. THE DAVID MODEL: CONSIDERING GOD'S CREATION AND MAJESTY

"Let the words of my mouth, and the meditation of my heart, be acceptable in thy sight, O Lord, my strength, and my redeemer." – Psalm 19:14

A. The revelation of God in nature:
1. _____Creation shows God_____. "The heavens declare the glory of God, and the firmament shows his handiwork." – Psalm 19:1
2. _____. "The voice of the Lord is upon the water." – Psalm 29:3
3. Questions to guide meditation: Who created the world? What did He create? When did He create? Why did He create? How did He create?

```
What Meditation Did for David

1.  It reminded him of God.
2.  It motivated him to worship God.
3.  It helped him understand his role in life.
4.  He sought forgiveness of God.
5.  He learned about God.
6.  He fellowshipped with God.
```

B. Ten Steps to Apply the David Model:
1. Observe _____.
2. Read the observations of _____.
3. Sing the _____ of the Christian faith.
4. Sing the _____.
5. Ask _____.
6. Write down _____ about God.
7. Apply thoughts to practical _____.
8. Move from meditation to _____.
9. Write in a journal your _____ and _____.
10. Start a _____ about your attitudes, values and personality.

III. THE MARY MODEL: PONDERING THE PERSON OF JESUS

"But Mary kept all these things and pondered them in her heart. – Luke 2:19

A. The attitude that led to Mary's meditation:
1. Mary was _____yield_____. – Luke 1:38
2. Mary was humble. – Luke 1:48, John 3:30
3. Mary was _____forgiven_____. – Luke 1:47
4. Mary was grateful. – Luke 1:49-50

> Gratitude is the least remembered of all virtues
> and
> Gratitude is the acid test of character

5. Mary was committed to ___excellence___. – Luke 1:28

> Because of our choices,
> we pursue a standard of excellence.
> And through our meditation
> We approach a life of excellence.

6. Mary was ___Committed to her son___. – John 2:5
7. Mary was ___satisfied___. – Luke 1:53

> **How to Ponder Jesus**
> 1. You meditate on Jesus' life.
> 2. You remember Jesus' death and resurrection.
> 3. You revisit your _Conversion experience_.
> 4. You ponder your salvation.

B. Ten steps to apply the Mary model:
1. Intentionally ___remember___
2. Become a ___note taker___
3. Make ___scrapbooks___
4. Sing ___hymns___ about Jesus
5. Sing praise ___choruses___
6. ___Memorize___ Scripture verses
7. ___View art___
8. Display ___Christmas nativity scenes___
9. Think through His ___lifeline___
10. Practice ___journaling___

IV. **THE ST. JOHN MODEL: THINKING ABOUT THE CROSS**
"Turn your whole attention to the results of the Father's love, it is that we are called the children of God." – 1 John 3:1, ELT

A. Meditating on the ___Cross___ of Christ.

B. How Saint John practiced meditation.
1. ___Look book___. – John 10:11

2. Remember the _____ of Christ's love. – Matt. 8:27
3. Identify the _____ of demonstrated love. – Matt. 6:13
4. Recognize the _____ of God's love. – Rom. 5:8
5. Receive _____ – John 19:26
6. Be _____ into God's family. – Matt. 2:23
7. Be _____ in God's love. – 1 John 3:2
8. Consider the _____ of the cross. – 1 John 3:1

C. Ten steps to apply the Saint John model:
1. Sing _____.
2. Practice _____ the cross.
3. View _____ to help focus on the cross.
4. Practice the _____.
5. _____ can direct your thinking to the cross.
6. Meditate on the _____ of His death.
7. Meditate on the _____.
8. Look at the cross _____.
9. _____ the cross to a particular sin.
10. Write down your _____ about the cross.

V. THE JOSHUA MODEL: FOCUSING ON BIBLICAL PRINCIPLES

"This book of the Law shall not depart from your mouth, but you shall meditate on it day and night, that you may observe all that is written in it. For then you will make your way prosperous, and then you will have good success." – Joshua 1:8

A. Principles for meditation that will make you successful:
1. Be successful on the ___inside___.

> **Three Excuses for Failure**
> 1. The competition is too big.
> 2. The circumstances are against me.
> 3. My background is inadequate.

2. Take ___responsibility___ for your growth and future achievement.
3. Follow ___good roll models___.
4. Commit yourself to the ___task___.
5. Learn to ___rise___ above your mistakes.
6. ___Do___ what you promise.
7. ___Discipline___ yourself to do what you have to do.
8. ___Prioritize___ your work and life.

> Do-what you have to do.

9. Give more to others than is ____expected____.
10. ____Believe____ in yourself.

B. Why meditate on Scriptures?
1. The Bible reveals the ____secrets____ of our hearts. – Rom. 3:9-20
2. The Scriptures reveal ____Jesus Christ____ to us. – Jn. 5:39
3. The Bible shows us how to have ____eternal life____ and be assured of it. – 1 Jn. 5:13
4. The Scriptures tell us God's ____expectation____ for our lives. – 2 Tim. 3:17
5. Knowing the Scriptures makes us ____smart____. – Jas. 1:5, Ps. 119:98-99
6. Meditating on Scriptures will provide ____spiritual power____. – 1 Cor. 10:13

> This Book will keep you from sin, or sin will
> keep you from this Book.
> -D. L. Moody

C. Ten Principles to take away:
1. Begin by ____Selecting____ a verse or verses for meditation.

> **How to Choose a Verse**
> 1. Meets a need in your life
> 2. Caught your attention during Bible reading
> 3. A promise you want to claim
> 4. A thought you want to keep/memorize
> 5. A life you want to follow
> 6. An attitude you need in your life
> 7. A promise of victory over a problem/sin

2. Study the ____context____ and ____cultural background____ to get the meaning of the passage.
3. Commit the verse(s) to ____memory____.
4. ____Paraphrase____ the passage to capture its meaning in your own words.
5. ____Define____ key words and phrases to gain greater insight.
6. Try to ____personalize____ the passage.
7. ____Pray____ the passage to God.
8. Think through the ____issues____ in the passage.
9. Use the great historic ____hymns____ in meditation.
10. Learn the new praise ____choruses____ for meditation

VI. THE ST. PAUL MODEL: BECOMING LIKE CHRIST

"If then you were raised with Christ, seek those things which are above, where Christ is, sitting at the right hand of God. Set your mind on things above, not on things on the earth." – Colossians 3:1-2

Character Steps to Being Like Christ

7. _Being like (Jesus) Christ_
6. Repeating
5. Doing
4. _Focusing_
3. Desiring
2. _Believing_
1. Thinking

A. Character steps to being like Christ:
1. *Thinking* – the first step to a changed life _begins with the mind_.
2. *Believing* – the Christian who wants to develop his or her faith in God must begin by learning the _basic facts of Scripture_.
3. *Desiring* – our _expectation or vision_ must come from God's Word.
   a. Five responses regarding the Christian life:
      1. Some never consider themselves as living for God – these have a _spiritual blindness_ problem.
      2. Some are aware of the Christian life but don't understand it – these have _a mental_ problem.
      3. Others know about the Christian life but never pursue it – these have a _problem of the will_.
      4. The fourth group endorses the Christian life but never feels it – these have _a heart problem_.
      5. The fifth group accepts the Christian life and through obedience achieves it – these have a _will to choose christ_.
   b. Four ways to grasp God's vision for your life:
      1. *Look* _within_ yourself to determine how God has enabled and gifted you.
      2. *Look* _behind_ yourself to see how God has used past events to shape you and prepared you for something greater.
      3. *Look* _around_ you to find examples you can follow.
      4. *Look* _ahead_ to determine where the Lord is leading in your life.
4. *Focusing* - people's attitudes are their _predispositions_ to life's focus.
   a. A new attitude develops new actions that _change our lives_.
   b. Four doors to developing new attitudes:
      1. Identify _the problem_ you wish to address.
      2. Know that _right thinking_ will lead to changing an emotional habit.

3. Relate to ____*positive people*____.
4. Develop ____*a plan*____ that will encourage positive attitudes and help develop a new habit.
5. *Doing* – my ____*Actions*____ earn me the right to communicate to others the kind of person I am.
6. *Repeating* – when we do something ____*regularly*____, it is either a habit or an accomplishment.
7. *Being like Christ* – you don't want to just *act like* Christ; you want to ____ *be like Christ*____.

B. Ten Principles to take away for meditation:
1. Make a _____ for change.

> ## St. Paul's Checklist for Meditation
> "Finally, brethren, whatever things are true, whatever things are noble, whatever things are just, whatever things are pure, whatever things are lovely, whatever things are of good report, if there is any virtue and if there is anything praiseworthy--meditate on these things." – Phil 4:8
> - Is it _____?
> - Is it _____?
> - Is it _____?
> - Is it _____?
> - Is it of _____?
> - Is there any _____ in it?
> - Is there anything _____ in it?

2. Read the _____ of others
3. Sing and _____ about the historic hymns of the faith.
4. Learn the new praise and worship choruses.
5. Make a list of _____ you desire.
6. Make a list of _____ you want to eliminate.
7. Pray for supernatural help.
8. Seek _____ help.
9. Develop your strengths.
10. Begin _____ down your progress.

VII. THE TIMOTHY MODEL: MEDITATING ON YOUR CALLING AND GIFTS
"Do not neglect the gift that is in you, which was given to you by prophecy with the laying on of the hands of the eldership. Meditate on these things; give yourself entirely to them, that your progress may be evident to all." – 1 Timothy 4:14-15

A. Five terms Paul used to describe spiritual gifts:
   1. *Pneumatikon*
      a. Translated "_____"
      b. Describes those gifts producing _____ in those receiving our ministry
   2. *Charismata*
      a. Translated "_____"
      b. Emphasizes that God gives gifts _____ and _____
   3. *Diakonia*
      a. Translated "_____"
      b. Reveals that our gifts _____ others
   4. *Energema*
      a. Translated "_____"
      b. Suggests gifts are an enduement of God's _____ and _____
   5. *Phanerosis*
      a. Translated "_____"
      b. Reveals that gifts are an _____ of God working through us

B. Steps to discerning God's will
   1. _____ yourself to God to do God's will.
   2. _____ the Bible.
   3. _____ for guidance on how to apply God's will.
   4. Make sure your motives are _____.
   5. Begin doing right.
   6. _____ your strengths and weaknesses realistically.
   7. Doing the will of God will result in an _____.
   8. Seek spiritual counsel from godly people.
   9. Walk through an open door to find God's will
   10. Don't move forward until you _____ you are following God's leading.
   11. Look at the _____ through God's eyes.
   12. _____ about your past decisions made regarding the will of God.

C. Ten principles to take away for meditation:
   1. _____."
   2. _____ about the call, commitment and obedience of other believers.
   3. Sing and meditate using the historic hymns of the Christian faith.
   4. The new praise and worship choruses will guide your meditation.
   5. Learn your spiritual giftedness.
   6. Ask _____ to help you identify your gift.
   7. Ask three revealing questions:
      a. Is this _____ with what I know about this gift?
      b. Is the _____ of this gift evident in my service and evident to other mature Christians I respect?

c. Is the _____ of this gift effective in ministry?
8. _____ till you find your spiritual gifts before you do something.
9. Begin demonstrating your gifts.
10. Begin today looking for articles, books, seminars, workshops and other opportunities to develop your spiritual gift(s).

VIII. THE HAGGAI MODEL: CONSIDERING YOUR FAILURES
"Now therefore, thus says the Lord of Hosts: 'Consider your ways!'" – Haggai 1:5

A. Consider your failures.
  1. It is not failures that hurt us; it is the way _We think_ about our failures that hurts us.
  2. Separate in your thinking the kinds of mistakes you make:
     a. _Intentional_ mistakes - mistakes we plan to make
     b. _Unintentional_ mistakes - mistakes we didn't mean to make, but we still have to pay the consequences.

B. Process for thinking about your mistakes:
  1. _Mess_ up
  2. _blow_ up
  3. _Cover_ up
  4. _back_ up
  5. _Slow_ up
  6. _Wake_ up
  7. Smell the _coffee_

C. Learning from our mistakes.
  1. The greatest mistake we can make in life is to be _afraid of mistakes_.
  2. Three things we can do with a mistake (Bear Bryant):
     a. _Admit_ it.
     b. _Learn_ from it.
     c. Don't _repeat_ it.
  3. Two types of people to avoid (Maxwell):
     a. The man who never makes a mistake, because _he is not honest_.
     b. The man who makes the same mistake twice, because _he is not learning_

D. How Haggai practiced meditation:
  1. Consider our _priorities_.
  2. Consider our _religious community_.
  3. We need to consider our _faith context_.

E. Ten steps to apply the Haggai Model:
  1. _Consider_ your failures and make a list of them.
  2. Ask yourself the three historic questions Haggai asked:
     a. What is the _purpose_ of living my life and what are my core values?

      b.   What do my ___relationships___ with others tell me about my relationship with God?

      c.   Are my actions ___consistent___ with the faith I profess in God?

  3.   Read ___practical books___ that will teach you principles to solve problems and overcome failures.

  4.   Search for historic hymns.

  5.   Search for new praise choruses.

  6.   Make a list of the ___biggest mistakes___ in life.

  7.   Make a ___list of lessons___ you learned from them.

  8.   Questions to consider:

      a.   What was the ___mistake___?

      b.   Why did I ___do it___?

      c.   How can I ___fix it___?

      d.   What did I ___learn from it___?

  9.   Share what you have learned with someone else.

 10.   Read of how ___others overcome___ failure and problems.

IX. THE ASAPH MODEL: MEDITATING ON GOD'S INTERVENTION

"In the day of my trouble I sought the Lord…and was troubled; I complained, and my spirit was overwhelmed. And I said, 'This is my anguish; but I will remember the years of the right hand of the Most High.' I will also meditate on all your work, and talk of your deeds." – Psalm 77:2-3, 10-12

A.   How Asaph practiced meditation:

  1.   In _____ turn to God.

  2.   Meditate on God's _____.

  3.   _____ what is meditated.

  4.   _____ what is meditated.

B.   The role of the Asaph Model in meditation:

  1.   It is one _____ to overcoming fear.

  2.   It is a _____ to serve God.

  3.   It results in our having _____ in the Scripture.

  4.   It is a call _____.

  5.   Meditating on the mighty works of God also gives us greater insight into the _____.

  6.   It gives us insight into the Scriptures.

  7.   Thinking about the way God has worked in your past stimulates you to a _____.

C.   Ten steps to apply the Asaph Model:

  1.   Read how _____ in history.

  2.   Read magazines, journals, letters and other written accounts.

  3.   _____ of Christian leaders also motivate people to meditate on God.

  4.   Historic hymns tell of God's intervention.

5. Sing the modern praise choruses.
6. Honestly express your feelings to God about your anxieties.
7. Focus on your meditation on what God has done for you.
8. Think through verses of promises and claim them.
9. Write a _____ testimony to share with others.
10. Keep a _____ of God's intervention in your life.

X. THE MALACHI MODEL: MEDITATING ON GOD'S NAMES

"Then those who feared the Lord spoke to one another, and the Lord listened and heard them; so a book of remembrance was written before Him for those who fear the Lord and who meditate on His name." – Malachi 3:16

A. Ten steps to apply the Malachi Model:
1. _____ God's name in speaking and writing.
2. Do not _____ using God's name or take His name in vain.
3. Use the historic hymns of the Christian faith to celebrate the names of God.
4. Learn the new praise and worship choruses.
5. Memorize a list of names for each Person of the Trinity.
6. Spend much time in _____ using God's many names.
7. Pray to God, use _____.
8. Use God's name in confession and repentance.
9. Recognize the uses of God's names.
10. Make a list of what you want to do through the power of God's name.

XI. THE KORAH MODEL: CONTEMPLATING INTIMACY WITH GOD

"We have thought, O God, on your lovingkindness, in the midst of Your temple."
– Psalm 48:9

A. Knowing God.
1. God, by His very nature, may be described as "_____."
2. By _____ God, we can celebrate His attributes and learn about Him.

B. How Korah practiced meditation:
1. Celebrate His _____.
2. Celebrate His _____.

C. Six principles for meditating on intimacy in 2 Corinthians 3:18 ("But we all, with unveiled face, beholding as in a mirror the glory of the Lord, are being transformed into the same image from glory to glory, just as by the Spirit of the Lord."):
1. Becoming like Christ is not a spiritual discipline _____.
2. Meditate as with an "_____," or takes steps to get rid of anything in our lives that may hinder our view of Christ.
3. Focus on a _____ of God.
4. "Behold as in a mirror," or looking at the attributes of God _____.

5. Being "transformed into the same image."
6. Yield to the Spirit's will and power to change us.

D. Ten steps to apply the Korah Model:
   1. Study the doctrines of God to know God.
   2. Look up verses for one attribute of God.
   3. Write down the biblical passages for one attribute of God.
   4. Write down everything you know about one aspect of God.
   5. Make a list of _____ that come from your meditation.
   6. Use the great hymns of the past to meditate on God.
   7. Use the new praise choruses to worship God.
   8. Write _____ of adoration/praise.
   9. Read devotional books.
   10. Begin a journal/diary.

Thy { name
{ kingdom
{ will
} Semi-Conclusion
} Hinge Bread
us { forgiving
{ lead
{ deliver
Conclusion.

CHAPTER ELEVEN
PRAYING THE LORD'S PRAYER

LESSON ONE

A. INTRODUCTION

(Taken from the book, *Praying the Lord's Prayer for Spiritual Breakthrough*, by Elmer Towns, Regal Books, Ventura, CA, 1997)

1. _To leave out nothing_. Story of Yonggi Cho.
2. _To pray for everything_. My daily activity.
3. _Used in many ways_. History of the Lord's Prayer.

B. WHY THE LORD'S PRAYER?

1. _Background_. Matthew 6:9-13, included in the Sermon On The Mount. In Luke 11:2-4, given after a disciple asked "teach us to pray." – Luke 11:1
2. _Pattern_. "After this manner."
   a. Can be prayed publicly, i.e., plural pronouns, us, our, we.
   b. Can be prayed privately, i.e., "enter into your closet." – Matt. 6:6

C. HOW TO BEGIN THE LORD'S PRAYER

1. _Unity_. The prayer begins with a plural pronoun "our," not a personal pronoun. God is not addressed as a Father, the Father, or my Father, but as "Our Father."
2. _Basis_. How do we come to God in prayer?
   a. Praying in Jesus' name. This is the way most prayers are concluded. "Whatsoever ye shall ask in my name that will I do" – John 14:14. But that formula is not found in the Lord's Prayer because it is included in the phrase "Our Father." We come to God with Jesus.
   b. Because of _Calvary_. We can pray the Lord's Prayer because we are covered by His blood shed at the cross. – Eph. 1:7
   c. Because of His _intercession_. We can pray the Lord's Prayer because "He (Jesus) ever liveth to make intercession for us." – Heb. 7:25
3. _Intimate_. A new title is given to God by Jesus. He is called Father. The title GOD (*Elohim*) means Creator, all-powerful Being. The title LORD (*Jehovah*) means the Self-Existent One, the covenant keeping Lord that relates to His people. The title MASTER (*Adonai*) means owner and/or possessor.

D. SEVEN PETITIONS OF THE LORD'S PRAYER

1. _Two sections_.

If we worship him, he will come.

pray is relationship.

THY PETITIONS: PRAYING FOR GOD'S GLORY "IN HEAVEN"
1. Thy name be hallowed.
2. Thy kingdom come.
3. Thy will be done.

Semi-Conclusion
~THE HINGE~
4. Give us our daily bread.

US PETITIONS: PRAYING FOR OUR SPIRITUALITY "ON EARTH"
5. Forgive us our debts.
6. Lead us not into temptation.
7. Deliver us from the Evil One.

Conclusion

2. *Semi – conclusion*. "On earth as it is in Heaven."
3. Overview of the seven petitions.

Worship	Hallowed Be Thy Name. A prayer for God to be glorified.
Guidance	Thy Kingdom Come. A prayer for God's principles to guide your life.
Yeld	Thy will be done. A prayer to submit to the rulership of God.
Provision	Give us this day our daily bread. A prayer for things to meet our daily needs.
Forgiveness	Forgive us our debts. A prayer to cleanse known and unknown sins.
Victory	Lead us not into temptation. A prayer for victory over sin and failure.
Protection	Deliver us from the Evil One. A prayer for protection from spiritual dangers and destruction.

LESSON TWO

A. INTRODUCTION

1. Illustration of Mount Rushmore.
2. *Worship God*. How to get God's presence in your life? God wants us to worship Him. "The Father is seeking such to worship Him." – John 4:23, NKJV. When we worship the Father, He will come to receive it. "The Lord is holy who dwells in the praises of Israel." – Ps. 22:3, author's translation

John 15: You in me ⇒ Position in christ in heaven
                         Right hand of the Father
         I in you ⇒ asking christ into our heart
                         indwelling

Five Essentials In Honoring God's Name

1. That God has a name.
2. That God's name is holy.
3. That God wants us to praise His name.
4. That I can praise His name with the Lord's Prayer.
5. That God will not force anyone to praise His name.

B. THAT GOD HAS A NAME

1. _____. What does the Towns name mean to me?
2. _____. You do not begin with your needs or your sins.
3. What do names/titles do for us?
   a. _____.
   b. _____.
   c. _____.
   d. _____.
4. _____. When you pray "Our Father, hallowed by Thy name," you recognize your relationship to Him.

C. GOD'S NAME IS HOLY

1. _____. What does the word *hallowed* mean?
2. _____. What are you doing when you hallow the name of God?
3. _____. How can you make God's name more hallowed in your life? By meditating on His nature and attributes.

Absolute Attributes	Comparative Attributes
Holiness	Omniscience
Love	Omnipresence
Justice	Omnipotence

4. When Moses prayed "Shew me thy glory" – Ex. 33:18, God answered, 'The Lord descended in a cloud and stood with Him there and proclaimed there the name of the Lord'" – Ex. 34:5. "And the Lord passed by before him, and proclaimed, the Lord, the Lord God, merciful and gracious, long-suffering and abundant in goodness and truth, keeping mercy for thousands, forgiving iniquity and transgression." – Ex. 34:6,7

D. GOD WANTS US TO PRAISE HIS NAME

1. _____. What does God need from us? God does not need our help, advice, service, or money. God wants our worship. "The Father is seeking such to worship Him." – John 4:23
2. _____. The Lord's Prayer is not primarily about getting things from God but properly relating to Him in fellowship.

E. I CAN WORSHIP WITH THE LORD'S PRAYER

1. _____. The greatest decision we can make each day is to worship God.
2. There are two approaches to God. First, _____. We can talk to God anywhere. We can say "Good morning, Lord." But there is a second approach. _____. There is a time to enter His presence with awe and anticipation. We come reverently to His presence with an offering of thanksgiving and praise.

F. GOD WILL NOT FORCE ANYONE TO WORSHIP HIM

1. God wants us to worship Him with our free will, "worship in spirit." – John 4:24
2. When we worship God correctly, "worship in truth" – John 4:24, we do it according to the Bible.

LESSON THREE

A. INTRODUCTION

1. _____. What is another title for God? "Harken unto the voice of my cry, my King, and my God: for unto thee will I pray." – Ps. 5:2
2. _____. What does kingship imply? Illustration of French Fries.

Five Essential Facts About God's Kingdom

1. God is our ruler – King.
2. God has a kingdom that He rules.
3. God's kingdom does not exist here and now.
4. God's kingdom can come here and now.
5. The Lord's Prayer can bring God's Kingdom.

B. GOD IS OUR RULER – KING

1. God is a _____. "Thou art my King, O God." – Ps. 44:4
2. As King, God has authority in the three areas of power:
   Legislature (Congress). God has _____.

Judicial   (Courts & Judges). God _____ disobedience.
           His people's response to His law.
Executive (President). God _____ His laws and His people.

C. GOD HAS A KINGDOM HE JUDGES

1. _____. When you pray "Thy kingdom come," you ask "God rule my heart."

2. _____. There is only one way to enter God's kingdom. "Except a man be born again, he cannot see the kingdom of God." – John 3:3

3. _____. Is God's kingdom outward? "Jesus answered, My kingdom is not of this world: if My kingdom were of this world, then would My servants fight . . . but now is My kingdom not from hence." – John 18:36

4. _____. If God's kingdom is not physical, where is it located? "For the kingdom of God is not meat and drink, but righteousness and peace, and joy in the Holy Ghost." – Rom. 14:17

D. GOD'S KINGDOM DOES NOT EXIST HERE AND NOW

1. _____. God intended to rule his people in the Old Testament. "If ye will obey my voice indeed, and keep my covenant, then ye shall be a peculiar treasure unto me above all people: for all the earth is mine: and ye shall be unto me a kingdom of priests, and an holy nation." – Ex. 19:5,6

2. _____. "They have rejected me that I should not rule over them." – I Sam. 8:7

3. _____. "Where is he that is born King of the Jews? For we have seen His star in the east, and are come to worship Him." – Matt. 2:2

4. _____. "He came unto his own, and his own received him not." – John 1:11 Crowned with thorns and hung a sign over his cross, "The King of the Jews."

> Characteristics of His Rule
> Inward . . . Invisible . . . Love
> Self discipline . . . Grace

E. GOD'S KINGDOM CAN COME HERE AND NOW

1. _____. For what are you asking when you pray? "Thy Kingdom come?"

2. _____. "But seek ye first the kingdom of God and his righteousness, and all these things shall be added unto you." – Matt. 6:33

3. _____. "If anyone wants to follow me, they must stop living for themselves and follow my principles daily." – Luke 9:23, author's translation

F. THE LORD'S PRAYER CAN BRING GOD'S KINGDOM

1. _____. If you pray, "Thy kingdom come," you can be the instrument to manifest God's rule on earth.
2. _____. If you pray, "Thy kingdom come," you will grow to be like Christ and learn to follow His example. "As ye have therefore received Christ Jesus the Lord, so walk ye in him." – Col. 2:6
3. _____. If you pray, "Thy kingdom come," you recognize the earth is not perfect as heaven.

GOD'S RULE IN HEAVEN

Right purpose, right motives, right timing,
right decisions. Right respect, right sensitivity,
right living, right standards.

LESSON FOUR

A. INTRODUCTION

1. Illustration of blue sign

God Has A Plan For Your Life

---

2. _____. Many people:
   a. Do not know that God has a plan for anyone.
   b. Do not know God has a plan for them.
   c. Have not attempted to find God's plan for them.

FIVE ESSENTIAL FACTS ABOUT GOD'S WILL

1. God has a plan for your personal life.
2. God's plan is good for you.
3. You can find and know God's plan now.
4. God will not force His plan on you.
5. The Lord's Prayer can help you find God's plan.

B. GOD HAS A PLAN FOR YOUR PERSONAL LIFE

1. Two views. First God's plan could be a _____. This is a noun, also described and pre-determined plan. Second, God's plan could be a _____. This could be a verb, also described as guidance.

2. Different expressions of God's will.
    a. _____. His laws run the universe.
    b. _____. What God wants done. "He is not willing that any should perish, but that all should come to repentance." – II Peter 3:9
    c. _____. What God expects, "Be ye holy." – I Peter 1:16
3. _____. God expects us to know His will. Paul told us, "Be ye not unwise, but understanding what the will of the Lord is." – Eph. 5:17

C. GOD'S PLAN IS GOOD FOR YOU

1. _____. "Be not influenced by this world but be supernaturally changed by a new way of thinking so you can do the will of God that is good, and appropriate and perfect." – Rom. 12:2, author's translation
2. _____. The request, "Thy will be done" is an aorist verb, which means point action.

D. YOU CAN FIND AND DO GOD'S WILL NOW

1. _____. Who should sit on the throne of your life? "For to me to live is Christ." – Phil. 1:21
2. _____. The Christian life is one big **YES,** followed by a daily small **yes.**

```
┌─────────────────────────────────┐
│          FOUR PRAYERS           │
│                                 │
│   1. Help me find Thy plan.     │
│   2. Help me understand Thy plan.│
│   3. Help me submit to Thy plan.│
│   4. Help me accomplish Thy plan.│
└─────────────────────────────────┘
```

E. GOD'S PLAN IS NOT FORCED ON ANYONE

1. _____. God runs His universe by laws; when we break a law, we suffer the consequences.
2. _____. Your prayer life begins with submission. "Prayer must change you, before it can change your circumstance."

F. THE LORD'S PRAYER CAN HELP US FIND GOD'S WILL

1. _____. "Prayer is a personal discipline that transforms us into a dedicated disciple."

2. Finding the plan of God comes two ways: First we find God's plan _____, like the dawning of a new day. Second, we find God's plan _____, like a light turned on in a dark room.

LESSON FIVE

A. INTRODUCTION – MATTHEW 6:9-13

1. _____. Illustration of tuna casserole.
2. _____. Bread stands for money, health, necessities, etc.
3. _____. We are to pray for bread (strength) so we can work for all the necessities of life. Don't have a lottery mindset nor look for God to support you by "mail box faith."

FIVE ESSENTIAL FACTS ABOUT OUR DAILY NEEDS

1. We have daily needs.
2. God will supply our needs.
3. We must ask God to supply our needs.
4. Our needs are supplied one day at a time.
5. We don't pray for everything, but we must pray about everything.

B. WE HAVE DAILY NEEDS

1. Salesman with hat.
2. _____. Most Americans do not need to pray, "Give us bread;" they need to pray, "Help me lose weight." However, some Americans are hungry.
3. _____. Why were we created to need food three times a day? God could have made us like rocks.
   _____.
   _____.
   _____.
   _____.

C. GOD WILL SUPPLY OUR NEEDS

1. _____. How should we eat? "Whether therefore you eat, or drink, or whatever you do, do all to the glory of God." – I Cor. 10:31
2. _____. When you daily ask God for bread, you are daily looking to God for everything. "Faith is affirming what God has said in His Word."

3. _____. The first three petitions relate to heaven: (1) Thy name be hallowed, (2) Thy kingdom come, (3) Thy will be done. You cannot fulfill these three without strength from daily bread.

D. WE MUST ASK GOD TO SUPPLY OUR NEEDS

1. _____. For what do we ask? How do we ask? We do not sit at the table and ask for food. We must work for it, cook it, serve it, and then eat it. "Prayer is declaring the majesty and purpose of God, then submitting my life to His will." God's will is that things grow, people work, that we plan our life by His rules for His glory.
2. _____. Some ask for too much, some for too little. Some ask for the lottery, others ask for a handout. "Prayer is more than what you ask and what you say; prayer is a way of life."

E. OUR NEEDS ARE SUPPLIED ONE DAY AT A TIME

1. _____. Praying "this day" you tell God you will walk with Him one day at a time.
2. _____. Praying "this day" you are not worried about the future. There is a difference between planning for the future and worrying about the future. _____. The ants are "exceedingly wise" because they "are a people not strong, yet they prepare their meat in summer." – Prov. 30:24,25
3. _____. Before you ask, "Your Father knoweth what things ye have need of before ye ask Him." – Matt. 6:8
4. _____. "Give me neither poverty nor riches, feed me with food convenient for me" – Prov. 30:8. Illustration of convenience store that has convenient bread. "Lest I be full, and deny thee, and say, 'Who is the Lord?' Or lest I be poor, and steal, and take the name of my God in vain." – Prov. 30:9

F. WE DO NOT PRAY FOR EVERYTHING, BUT WE PRAY ABOUT EVERYTHING

1. God runs the world by His _____. We do not just pray for water to boil; we put it on the fire. We work for good, but pray about our work.

   _____.
   _____.
   _____.
   _____.
   _____.

2. Praying is never wrong, but sometimes our prayers are wrong.
    Wrong _____.
    Wrong _____.
    Wrong _____.
    Wrong _____.

LESSON SIX

A. INTRODUCTION

1. _____. This prayer is not for initial forgiveness. If you have already called God your Father, then you are a Christian.
2. _____. This prayer is not about dying outside of Christ.
3. _____. This prayer is not about our relationship to God, but about our fellowship with God.
4. _____. What was Johnny's problem in the illustration of the goose?

FIVE ESSENTIAL FACTS ABOUT OUR SIN

1. God's children sin.
2. God's children are concerned after they sin.
3. God's children must do something about their sin.
4. God will forgive them.
5. Forgiving others is essential.

B. GOD'S CHILDREN SIN

1. _____. What is God's standard for His children? "Be ye perfect." – Matt. 5:48. "My little children, these things write I unto you, that ye sin not." – I John 2:1
2. _____. How many of God's children break His rules? "All have sinned." – Rom. 3:23
3. How many ways do we displease the Father?
    a. _____. Father asks son to wash car. He did not.
    b. _____. Treat the car as I would treat it.
    c. _____. Son never comes to family events, trips, etc.
4. _____. When you ask, "Forgive us our debts" you are asking God to forgive any and every disobedience.

C. GOD'S CHILDREN ARE CONCERNED AFTER THEY SIN

1. _____. What was the problem in the illustration of the Chinese girl?
2. You can sin _____ or _____. So pray "Forgive us our debts."

3. _____. Simply praying the Lord's Prayer is not enough. "For godly sorrow worketh repentance." – II Cor. 7:10. Godly sorrow is meaning you are so sorry, you will never want to do it again.

D. GOD'S CHILDREN MUST DO SOMETHING ABOUT THEIR SIN

1. _____. What accompanies the Lord's Prayer? "If we confess our sins, He is faithful and just to forgive us our sins." – I John 1:9
2. _____. The prayer "Forgive us our debts" must be followed by actions. The prodigal son first changed his mind, "Came to himself" – Luke 15:17, then made a decision, "I will arise and go to my father." – Luke 15:18. Finally, he repented, i.e., changed his actions. "And he arose, and came to his father." – Luke 15:20

E. GOD WILL FORGIVE THEM

1. _____. What is the greatest quality of God? "Who is a God like unto thee, that pardoneth iniquity, and passeth by the transgression of the remnant . . .? He . . . delighteth in mercy. He will turn again, He will have compassion upon us, . . . Thou wilt cast all their sins into the depths of the sea." – Micah 7:18,19
2. _____. When will God forgive our sins? "Behold the Lamb of God that taketh away the sin of the world." – John 1:29

> The Father already has forgiven us.
> He wants to deliver us.

F. FORGIVING OTHERS IS ESSENTIAL

1. _____. This is our original conversion that establishes a relationship with God. He becomes our Father because we become His children – John 1:12.
2. _____. When believers confess their sins, they reestablish a child-father relationship with God.
3. Three pictures.
   a. Forgiveness is like a _____. You must have both a ticket and receipt to fly.
   b. Forgiveness is like a _____. What goes around, comes around. You must forgive others to get forgiveness in life.
   c. Forgiveness is an expression of _____. To be loved, we must love.

> Gratitude is the least remembered of all virtues, but is the acid test of character.

LESSON SEVEN

A. INTRODUCTION – MATTHEW 6:9-13

1. Illustration: The danger of a snake.
2. _____. Pray "lead us not into temptation" when you want victory, and even when you do not want victory. Prayer may change your desire.

FIVE ESSENTIAL FACTS ABOUT TEMPTATION

1. God allows His children to be tempted.
2. God's children can fall.
3. God expects His children to overcome temptation.
4. The Lord's Prayer can help overcome temptation.
5. There is a life of victory.

B. GOD ALLOWS HIS CHILDREN TO BE TEMPTED

1. Opportunity knocks only once, temptations _____.
2. The Lord is our leader. "The Lord is my shepherd . . . He leadeth me." – Ps. 23:1,2
   a. You are not praying _____.
   b. You are not praying _____. "Let no man say when he is tempted, I am tempted of God, for God cannot be tempted with evil, neither tempteth he any man." – James 1:13
   c. You are not praying _____. Because that denies the type of world where we live.
3. _____. The nature of life is that we are given a test to determine our character and our destination.
4. _____. This is not a head prayer. You are saying, "I have been there and I do not want to go there again."
5. Illustration: Driver of car says to person with the map, "Do not let me take the wrong turn."

C. GOD'S CHILDREN CAN FALL

1. Lead me not into temptation, _____.
2. _____. Every child is "Beauty and the Beast," each has a good nature and evil nature. We are tempted, "When he (we) are drawn away by his own lust and enticed." – James 1:14b
3. _____. Satan will lay a trap for us, "Love not the world . . . For all that is in the world, the lust of the flesh, and the lust of the eyes, and the pride of life, is not of the Father but is of the world." – I John 2:15,16

4. _____. "If we say that we have no sin (sin nature) we deceive ourselves." – I John 1:8. "If we say that we have not sinned (continual acts of sin) we make Him a liar, and His word is not in us." – I John 1:10

D. GOD EXPECTS HIS CHILDREN TO OVERCOME TEMPTATION

1. _____. Not to flunk us, but to approve us.
2. _____. "Now unto Him who is able to keep you from falling." – Jude 24
3. _____. "This is the victory that overcometh the world." – I John 5:4

E. THE LORD'S PRAYER CAN HELP OVERCOME TEMPTATION

1. _____. In the garden, Jesus instructed, "Watch and pray that ye enter not into temptation, the spirit indeed is willing, the flesh is weak" – Matt. 26:41
2. _____. When you pray, you are asking for deliverance from a crisis of a specific evil temptation and from the place of evil where you will be continually tempted. *Prosmos* (temptation) has continuous action in the original language.
3. _____. You are praying for deliverance today and all future days.
4. _____. After this prayer, "flee these things." – I Tim. 6:11
5. _____. The Christian life is like school; when we pass a test, it qualifies us for a more difficult test.

F. A LIFE OF VICTORY

1. _____. "There hath no temptation taken you but such as is common to man, but God is faithful, who will not suffer you to be tempted above that ye are able; but will with the temptation also make a way to escape, that ye may be able to bear it." – I Cor. 10:13
2. _____. Jesus prayed for us, "I pray not that Thou shouldest take them out of this world, but that Thou shouldest keep them from the evil one." – John 17:15

LESSON EIGHT

A. INTRODUCTION

1. _____. The *King James* states "Deliver us from evil" but the modern versions state, "Deliver us from the Evil One." Who is this?

2. _____. What is Satan's purpose with the believer? "Be sober, be vigilant, because your adversary, the Devil, as a roaring lion, walketh about, seeking whom he may devour." – I Peter 5:8

FOUR ESSENTIAL FACTS ABOUT THE EVIL ONE

1. Evil One exists.
2. The Evil One is in spiritual conflict with you.
3. God is your deliverer.
4. You can use the Lord's Prayer for deliverance.

B. THE EVIL ONE EXISTS

1. _____. What is one of the essential lessons that is taught to a soldier in boot camp?
2. _____. How can you describe the Christian life? "We wrestle not against flesh and blood, but against principalities and powers, against the ruler of the darkness of this world, against spiritual wickedness in high places." – Eph. 6:12
3. _____. Satan does not want us to know about him. He will lie to us and deceive us. Jesus called him, "A liar . . . the father of lies" – John 8:44. "The great dragon . . . that old serpent, called the Devil and Satan, which deceiveth the whole world." – Rev. 12:9
   a. Costume, with red suit and pitchfork.
   b. Growing influence of occult and Satan worshippers.
   c. Deny supernatural and Devil.

C. THE EVIL ONE IS IN CONFLICT WITH US

1. _____. What should be our attitude knowing the Evil One wants to destroy us?

"Greater is He that is in you, than he that is in the world." – I John 4:4

---

2. How does Satan attack us?
   a. _____. "Then cometh the Devil, and taketh away the word out of their hearts, lest they should believe and be saved." – Luke 8:12
   b. _____. "In whom the god of this world hath blinded the minds of them which believe not, lest the light of the glorious gospel of Christ, who is the image of God, should shine unto them." – II Cor. 4:4
   c. _____. "False prophets . . . transforming themselves into the apostles of Christ. And no marvel, for Satan himself is transformed into an angel of light. Therefore, it is no great thing if his ministers also be transformed as the ministers of righteousness." – II Cor. 11:13-15

d. _____. "Simon, behold Satan hath desired to have you, that he may sift you as wheat." – Luke 22:31

D. GOD IS YOUR DELIVERER

1. _____. What is provided for the believer?

> "There hath no temptation taken you but such as is common to man: but God is faithful, who will not suffer you to be tempted above that ye are able; but will with the temptation also make a way to escape, that ye may be able to bear it." – I Cor. 10:13

2. What should be our principles to defeat Satan?
   a. _____. We must fear God. – Deut. 31:12
   b. _____. A wise Christian will not "hang around" sin and temptation. "Abstain from all appearance of evil" – I Thess. 5:22. "Flee these things." – I Tim. 6:11.
   c. _____. "Submit yourselves unto God. Resist the devil, and he will flee from you" – James 4:7. "Resist steadfastly in the faith." – I Peter 5:9.
   d. _____. Boy Scouts have a motto, "Be Prepared." The Christian should, "Watch and pray, lest ye enter into temptation." – Mark 14:38. "Put on the whole armour of God, that ye may be able to stand against the wiles of the devil." – Eph. 6:11

E. USE THE LORD'S PRAYER FOR DELIVERANCE

1. _____. The illustration of a camp speaker in an accident.
2. _____. The illustration of the Holiday Inn window.
3. _____. "The Lord shall preserve thee from all evil . . . the Lord shall preserve thy going out and thy coming in." – Ps. 121:7,8

CHAPTER TWELVE
PRAYER

"Nothing of eternal consequence happens apart from prayer. Churches grow when people pray effectively to get people saved, receive resources, remove barriers and enrich the service of Christ."

"There are two kinds of means requisite to promote a revival: the one to influence God, the other to influence men. Prayer is an essential link in the influence that leads to a revival, as much so as truth is. Some have zealously used truth to convert men, and laid very little stress on prayer. They have preached, and talked, and distributed tracts with great zeal, and then wondered that they had so little success. And the reason was that they forgot to use the other branch of the means, effectual prayer. They overlooked the fact that truth, by itself, will never produce the effect, without the Spirit of God, and that the Spirit is given in answer to prayer." – Charles G. Finney

A. WHAT IS PRAYER?

1. *Proseuchomai* – Prayer that is directed ___to God___. – Phil. 1:9; Eph. 6:18; Heb. 13:8
2. *Aiteo* – Prayer that makes a ___request to God___. – Matt. 7:7
3. *Deomai* – Prayer that expresses a ___deep desire___ or need. – Luke 10:2; 22:32
4. *Epikaleo* – Prayer that ___calls upon God___ for help. – Acts 7:59; Rom. 10:13
5. *Entunchano* – Prayer that ___pleads___ with God for results. – Rom. 8:27; 11:2; Heb. 7:25
6. *Enteuxis* – Prayer that requests ___favor from a sovereign God___ God. – 1 Tim. 2:1; 4:5

B. SEVEN KINDS OF PRAYER

1. Prayer of intercession ___for others___.
2. Prayer of worship ___for God___.
3. Prayer of agreement ___for communion___.
4. Prayer of petition ___for things___.
5. Prayer of confession ___for forgiveness___.
6. Prayer of salvation ___for sinners___.
7. Prayer of faith ___for miracles___.

C. WHAT ARE THE CONDITIONS OF PRAYER?

1. God responds to our prayer when we are ___yielded___ to Him. – Mark 14:36; 1 John 5:14
2. God responds to our prayer when we pray "___in Jesus___' name." – John 14:13, 14; 15:16

3. God responds to our prayer when we pray ___with faith___. – Heb. 11:6
4. God responds to our prayer when we are ___abiding in Christ___ and the Word of God. – John 15:7
5. God responds to our prayer when we are ___persistent___ in prayer. – Luke 18:1; Col. 4:2
6. God responds to our prayer when we pray ___humbly___. – Psalm 10:17; Luke 18:14
7. God responds to our prayer when we pray in ___sincerity___. – Psalm 145:18
8. God responds to our prayer when we are ___united___ with others in prayer. – Matt. 18:19; Acts 12:4
9. God responds to our prayer when we have a proper ___reverence___ for Him. – Psalm 145:19
10. God responds to our prayer when we pray with great ___intensity___. – Acts 12:4; Luke 22:44; Rom. 15:30; Col. 4:12

D. WHAT ARE THE HINDRANCES TO GETTING ANSWERS TO PRAYER?

1. Known or ___unconfessed sin___ will hinder the effectiveness of our prayers. – Psalm 66:18; Isa. 59:1,2
2. Rejecting the ___clearly revealed___ will of God will hinder the effectiveness of our prayers. – 1 Sam. 8:18; Prov. 28:9
3. Praying with a ___wrong motive___ will hinder the effectiveness of our prayers. – James 4:3
4. ___Harboring idols___ will hinder the effectiveness of our prayer. – Ezek. 14:3
5. An ___unforgiving spirit___ will hinder the effectiveness of our prayer. – Mark 11:25, 26
6. Failure to respond to the needs of the poor will hinder the effectiveness of our prayer. – Prov. 21:13
7. ___Domestic conflict___ will hinder the effectiveness of our prayer. – 1 Peter 3:7

E. INTERCESSORY PRAYER

Intercessory prayer is God's all-powerful agency for the outpouring of the Spirit. No revival has ever yet been given apart from this ministry. – Oswald J. Smith

1. ___Communion, petition, and intercession___.
   a. Communion prayers are "talking with God" about things of common concern, but not necessarily making specific requests for divine intervention.
   b. Petition prayers are asking or requesting prayers.
   c. Intercession is an outgrowth of the communion and petition prayers and reaches out on behalf of others.

2. ___Identification, agony and authority___.
   a. The intercessor identifies himself with the one for whom he was praying just as Jesus numbered Himself among the transgressors.

b. The intercessor agonizes in prayer as Jesus agonized in the garden of Gethsemane.

c. The intercessor prays with authority knowing he can and will influence God with his prayer.

3. Intercession as ___redemptive___.
   a. Moses offered himself for his people. – Ex. 32:31, 32; Psalm 106:23
   b. Jesus offered Himself after praying for His people. – John 17; Heb. 5:7-9
   c. Paul wished he could have given himself for his people. – Rom. 9:3

4. Intercession as ___Christian service___.

   The highest form of Christian service – Oswald J. Smith

   It helps greatly to remember that intercession is service: the chief service of a life on God's plan. It is unlike all other forms of service, and superior to them in this: that it has fewer limitations. – S. D. Gordon

5. Praying for the ___pastor___. – cf. Col. 4:2-4
   a. Pray that God will open doors of opportunity.
   b. Pray that the pastor will effectively communicate the Gospel as he has opportunity to do so.

   The preachers who have been most widely used have been men of prayer. Not only have they prayed themselves, but it will generally be found that others were linked with them in this precious service, and many of these prayer-evangelists have never been brought to public notice. – H. A. Ironside

   It is absolutely necessary for the preacher to pray. It is an absolute necessity that the preacher is prayed for. These two propositions are wedded into a union, which ought never to know any divorce: the preacher must pray; the preacher must be prayed for. It will take all the praying he can do, and all the praying he can get done, to meet the fearful responsibilities and gain the largest, truest success in his great work. – E. M. Bounds

6. Praying for the ___unsaved___. – John 17:20
   a. Each person must make his/her own decision for Christ and there is nothing we can do to force God to act contrary to a person's will in saving them.
   b. We can invite the Holy Spirit to work in a person's life so as to make them more receptive and responsive to the Gospel.
   c. It is doubtful if many people have ever been saved without someone first praying for that person's salvation.

7. Praying for ___missions___.
   a. We should pray for more laborers. – Matt 9:38
   b. We should pray for the missionaries who have already gone out. – Col. 4:2-4

c. We should pray for the outpouring of the Spirit on different fields.
d. We should pray for the national Christians.
e. We should pray for the national churches.
f. We should pray for the secretaries and official members of the various boards here at home.
g. We should pray for money.

8. Intercession as _Christian experience_.
   a. Jesus is engaged in intercession. – Heb. 7:25
   b. The Holy Spirit is an intercessor. – Rom. 8:26
   c. "To engage in this same ministry is to do down here what Christ is doing up there." – Oswald J. Smith

9. How to engage in intercessory prayer.
   a. Be certain there is nothing in your walk with God that might _____ _hinder your prayer_.
   b. Develop an "_others_" attitude and emphasis in your prayer.
   c. Develop your _faith in God_ so as to be able to pray until an answer comes.
   d. Be prepared for _His will_.

F. PREVAILING IN PRAYER

To prevail is "to be successful in the face of difficulty, to completely dominate, to overcome and triumph." Prevailing prayer is prayer that pushes right through all difficulties and obstacles, drives back all the opposing forces of Satan, and secures the will of God. Its purpose is to accomplish God's will on earth. Prevailing prayer is prayer that not only takes the initiative but continues on the offensive for God until spiritual victory is won. – Wesley L. Duewel

1. The _necessity_ of prevailing prayer.
2. We must prevail in prayer to overcome Satan in his battle for the souls of men and attempt to corrupt and confuse the believer. – 1 Chron. 21:1; Matt. 16:33; Luke 9:55-56
3. We should also prevail in prayer for ourselves in this regard. – 2 Cor. 12:7
4. Prevailing prayer is the human means of obtaining spiritual power for ministry – Luke 11:13– and other blessings from God such as revival. – cf. Luke 18:1-8
   a. The _objective_ in prevailing prayer.
      1. We need to prevail against the weakness of the flesh. – Matt. 26:41
      2. We need to prevail against Satan in a spiritual conflict for the souls of men. – cf. John 14:30; Eph. 2:2; 6:11-12; 1 John 4:4; 5:19
      3. There are times when we must prevail before God because God wants to test the sincerity of our prayer before He responds with a quick answer. – cf. Matt. 15:21-28
   b. How to prevail in prayer.

1. You must be willing to ___*send much time*___ in prayer (cf. Daniel, Nehemiah).
2. You must build a ___*reservoir of prayer*___, which means praying in the power of the Holy Spirit and in accordance with His will and leading. – Eph. 6:18; Jude 20
3. You must pray with a sense of ___*determination*___. – Matt. 7:7
4. Prevailing prayer also involves praying with ___*your whole being*___. – Jer. 29:13
5. You must pray with ___*great intensity*___ when you prevail in prayer. – Rom. 15:30

G. HOW CAN A PASTOR LEAD HIS CHURCH TO PRAY AND EXPECT ANSWERS?

1. Only a ___*praying pastor*___ can build a praying church.
2. Identify a ___*group of praying people*___ who can provide leadership in a prayer movement.
3. Pray! Ask God to give others your burden for prayer.
4. Be faithful in teaching your people ___*about prayer*___.
5. Publish and distribute a church ___*prayer list*___.
6. Establish an ___*accountability network*___ to encourage people to keep praying.
7. Promote prayer in connection with ___*other projects*___ of the church.
8. Appoint a ___*prayer coordinator*___ in the church who will accept the responsibility of leading this ministry and keeping it on track.
9. Establish a prayer relationship between pastor and people.

CHAPTER THIRTEEN
THE CHANGE THAT SALVATION
MAKES IN AN INDIVIDUAL

A. The Plan of Salvation.

In the work of regeneration, the soul is ___passive___. It cannot cooperate in the communication of spiritual life. But in conversion, repentance, faith and growth in grace, all its ___powers___ are exercised. Salvation appears to be very complicated; salvation is really as simple as a relationship with Jesus Christ. Charles Haddon Spurgeon was saved as he heard a Methodist layman preach on the text, "Look . . . and be . . . saved." – Isa. 45:22

1. Knowledge of the ___need___ of salvation. "For all have sinned, and come short of the glory of God." – Rom. 3:23
2. Knowledge of the ___penalty___ of sin. "For the wages of sin is death; but the gift of God is eternal life through Jesus Christ our Lord." – Rom. 6:23
3. Knowledge of ___God's provision___. "But God commendeth His love toward us, in that, while we were yet sinners, Christ died for us." – Rom. 5:8
4. Man must ___respond___ to the Good News. "That if thou shalt confess with thy mouth the Lord Jesus, and shalt believe in thine heart that God hath raised him from the dead, thou shalt be saved." – Rom. 10:9

B. The Gospel.

1. The Gospel has two aspects: ___propositional___ truth and ___personal___ truth.
2. Propositional truth reflects the truth in theoretical principles and written in our doctrinal statements.
3. "I declare unto you the gospel which I preached unto you . . . that Christ died for our sins according to the scriptures; and that He rose again the third day according to the scriptures." – I Cor. 15:1-4
4. The Gospel explains the death, burial and resurrection of Jesus Christ.
5. The Gospel is a personal truth that exists in a person, i.e., ___Jesus Christ___.
6. The Gospel becomes personal when you invite Christ into your life.
7. "But to as many as received Him (Christ), to them gave He power to become the sons of God." – John 1:12

C. Conversion.

1. The term conversion may be one of the most misunderstood religious terms in popular use today. Often the concepts of conversion and regeneration are used interchangeably.
2. Conversion is the ___human side___ of that experience in which regeneration is the ___divine side___.

3. A second more serious erroneous view of conversion is to define it exclusively in terms of "a stimulus-response, i.e., _a psychological experience_ .

4. What is biblical conversion? The "conversion" means a "turning _from sin to God_ on the part of the sinner.

"Conversion is the word employed in theology to designate the turning of a sinner from his sins unto Christ for his salvation. This includes both the forsaking of sin which we have defined as _repentance_ , and the trust in Christ which we have defined as _faith_ ." – Edgar Young Mullins

---

"Conversion is that voluntary change in the mind of the sinner, in which he turns, on the one hand from sin, and on the other hand to Christ. The former or negative element in conversion, namely the turning from sin, we dominate _repentance_ . The _later of positive element in conversion_ , namely the turning to Christ, we _denominate faith_ ." – Strong (p. 829)

---

5. "Ye have obeyed from the heart that form of doctrine which was delivered you." – Rom. 6:17

A. Intellect

It is imperative to know both the content (doctrine) and the Person (Jesus Christ) of the Gospel to be converted.

B. Emotions

"Not that ye were made sorry, but that ye sorrowed to repentance: for ye were made sorry after a godly manner . . . for godly sorrow worketh repentance to salvation not to be repented of: but the sorrow of the world worketh death." – II Cor. 7:9-10

Each person has a different way of expressing emotions, depending on age, sex, background, and a host of other unique experiences that make us who we are.

C. Will

The Will and Conversion	
1. Trust in	Prov. 3:4
2. Repent	Acts 2:38
3. Believe	Acts 16:31
4. Receive	John 1:12
5. Be born again	John 3:7
6. Call	Rom. 10:13
7. Confess	Rom. 10:9

"When is a child old enough to be converted?" The discussion hinges upon "_____ _the age of acauntability_____." A Jewish boy becomes "a son of the covenant" on his twelfth birthday; when a child is old enough to recognize the existence of God and his claims upon his life and to know he is a sinner.

D. Repentance

1. Some object to including repentance as part of the doctrine of salvation because they believe it suggests a doctrine of salvation _works_____.
2. Repentance is necessary for salvation, but repentance _does not save one____.
3. Like the bus ticket that says, "This half good for passage, not good if detached." This ticket stub represents repentance: not good for passage to Heaven; keep doing good until you get to your destination.
4. Repentance means to change one's mind about sin in such a way as to eventually effect _a change in the way of life_____.
5. "Repentance is that voluntary change in the mind of the sinner in which he turns from sin. Being essentially a change of mind, it involves a change of view, a change of feeling, and a change of purpose." – Strong
6. Repentance includes three elements:
    a. First, there is an intellectual element. It is a change of _thought_____.
    b. There is also a change of feeling. Regret is of a godly kind, which leads to a _real change_____.
    c. There is also a voluntary element in genuine _repentance_____.
7. Two Greek words are translated repentance. The most common of these two terms is *metonoia* meaning "a change of mind or thought." The second word for repentance is *metamelomai*. According to Mullins, "This word expresses the emotional elements in repentance. It means regret."
8. Charles Finney was generally opposed to emotional outbursts during his meetings. As a trained lawyer, his conservative nature revolted at the thought of individuals interrupting his sermons, crying out over the condition of their souls. As a result, Finney instituted "_the anxious seat_____."
9. The Thessalonian Christians "turned to God from idols, to serve the living and true God." – I Thess. 1:9
10. Some have argued that John and Paul differed on the importance of repentance in conversion. While it is true John never uses the word repent in any of his writings, his use of the word believer demands _active obedience_____ to that which is held to be true, thus implying repentance.

E. Faith

1. Repentance falls short of salvation without _saving faith_____.
2. Faith is as simple as a drowning man reaching for a rope, a child taking a step, or a sinner looking to Jesus Christ.
3. Faith means abandoning all trust _in one's own resources___. Faith means casting oneself unreservedly _on the mercy of God_____.

4. The closest thing to a biblical definition of faith is "the substance of things hoped for, the evidence of things not seen." – Heb. 11:1

5. Six different uses of the term "faith" in scriptures:

   a. When faith is used with an article, as in the faith, it is a reference to the scriptures or ___doctrinal faith___.

   b. There is ___saving faith___.

   c. There is a non-experiential faith that is described as ___justifying faith___. – Rom. 3:27-31

   d. The fourth is ___indwelling faith___, which seems to be the active faith of Christ that indwells the believer and gives him the ability to trust in God. – Mark 11:22

   e. The ___daily faith___ of the believer, which is living by the principles of God's word. – II Cor. 5:7

   f. The sixth is ___the gift of faith___, which is a spiritual gift that the believer has to move obstacles that hinder the work of Christ. – I Cor. 12:9; 13:2

6. ___Knowledge___ is the basis for volitional faith. In the first step, the person believes in the existence of God, that the Bible is God's Word, that Jesus has shed His blood on the cross for the sins of mankind, and that God will save those who call upon Him. This knowledge is not ultimate faith, but is the beginning.

7. Saving faith is not a ___leap___ in the dark. It is based upon objective truth.

8. The verb *pisterio* is often followed by "that," indicating that faith is concerned ___facts___.

9. Faith also involves the feeling of man, as either ___cause of effect___.

10. This emotional element of faith, though valid in its place, is often abused or overemphasized by evangelists.

11. In one sense, the human will must act in faith. On the other hand, faith comes to those who cease self-effort.

12. Saving faith is the verb *pisterio*, which is followed by the preposition *eis*. Literally this means "to believe into."

13. Faith is not accepting certain things as true, but trusting a Person, and ___knowing certain things are true___.

F. Justification

1. One of the most important questions ever asked in the history of mankind is, "How can a man be justified with God?" – Job 9:2; 25:4

2. Justification is ___an act___ whereby our legal standing in Heaven is changed and man is given a new standing before God.

3. By justification we mean that judicial act of God by which, on account of Christ, to whom the sinner is united by faith, he declares that sinner to be no longer exposed to the penalty of the law, but to be ___restored to divine favor___.

4. It is ___imputed righteousness___. It is not that man has become perfect, only that God has declared him righteous.

5. Abraham is the first person in the Bible described as having been justified by faith. "He (Abraham) believed in the Lord, and He (God) counted it to him (Abraham) for righteousness." – Gen. 15:6

G. Regeneration

1. Regeneration is used only once in Scripture where Paul speaks of "the washing of regeneration." – Titus 3:5

2. Regeneration may be defined as the change *one's moral disposition* wrought by the Spirit of God.

3. Regeneration is accomplished through the instrumentality of *the Word of God*.

4. Regeneration, or the new birth, is the *divine side* of that change of heart which, viewed from the *human side*, we call conversion.

5. Regeneration is the work of God through the Holy Spirit, of placing in one who has faith, *a new nature* capable of doing the will of God.

6. Regeneration gives the believer *new desires* to do the will of God (new nature) and gives him the life of God.

7. The initiative in regeneration is ascribed to God. – John 1:13

8. Man is *given new powers and new attitudes* in the new birth; God acts on him.

9. When a person is born again – John 1:12-13, the indwelling presence of *Jesus Christ* comes into his life.

10. *The Father* also indwells the believer, "We will come unto him and make our abode with him." – John 14:23

11. *The Holy Spirit* also indwells the Christian, "by His Spirit that dwelleth in you." – Rom. 8:11

12. A person becomes a new creation.

13. In regeneration a person receives a *life of God* with new power and new attitude.

14. Regeneration is not a physical change.

15. Regeneration is giving a new direction or tendency to powers of affection which man possessed before.

16. The *agent* of regeneration. The Holy Spirit is the Person who grants eternal life to the repentant sinner.

17. The *instrument* of regeneration. The Bible is the instrument that God uses in an individual's regeneration. We are "born again, not of corruptible seed, but of incorruptible, by the Word of God, which liveth and abideth forever." – I Peter 1:23

18. Summary of regeneration.
    a. *Given eternal life*.
    b. New nature.
    c. *New desires and new powers*.
    d. Member of God's family.

H. Union with Christ

1. Union with Christ is that judicial placing of a believer "in Christ" in *the heavens*, so that there is an accomplished union between the two.

2. One of the unique expressions of Paul is " *In Christ* ."

3. There is no condemnation to those who are "in Christ" – Rom. 8:1. Christians are alive unto God "in Christ Jesus" – Rom. 6:11. If any man is "in Christ," he is a new

creature." – II Cor. 5:17. Paul declared that he had been crucified and that Christ lived in him. – Gal. 2:20. We are baptized "into Christ." – Gal. 3:27. Christ dwells in the heart by faith – Eph. 3:17. We are created "in Christ Jesus unto good works." – Eph. 2:10

4. Another Pauline expression teaching the doctrine of union with Christ is the word, "together."

The Seven Togethers

1. Crucified together with Christ – Gal. 2:20 - συνεσταύρωμαι.
2. Died together with Christ – Col. 2:20 - συναπεθανετε
3. Buried together with Christ – Rom. 6:4 - συνεταφημεν
4. Quickened together with Christ – Eph. 2:5 - συνεζωοποιησεν
5. Raised together with Christ – Col. 3:1 - συνηγερθητε.
6. Suffer together with Christ – Rom. 8:17 - συμπασχομεν
7. Glorified together with Christ – Rom. 8:17 - συνδοξαεθωμεν – Strong

---

5. This doctrine is taught in Scripture by the use of five biblical illustrations:
   (1) A ___building___ and its foundation. – Eph. 2:20-22; I Peter 2:4-5
   (2) The union of ___husband and wife___. – Eph. 5:31-32
   (3) The vine and the ___branches___. – Jn. 15:1-10
   (4) The ___body___; Christ is the head, and believers are members of the body. – I Cor. 6:15; 12:12
   (5) The ___human race___ and its source in its head Adam. – Rom. 5:12-21

6. What our union with Christ produces:
   a. An ___organic___ union – we become members of Christ.
   b. A ___vital___ union – Christ's life becomes the dominating principle within us.
   c. A ___spiritual___ union – author is the Holy Spirit.
   d. An ___indissoluble___ union – can never be dissolved.
   e. An ___inscrutable___ union – surpassing in its intimacy and value any other union of the soul which we know.

I. Sanctification

1. The verb, to sanctify means "to set apart," and the noun sanctification means, literally, separation.
2. The word "sanctification" is used in the Bible to identify a person, institution, act, or thing used by God as holy.
3. Sanctification for the Christian is past, present, and future, or positional, progressive and prospective sanctification.
   a. ___Positional___ sanctification is the relationship with God, which we enter by faith in Jesus Christ. What God made holy by redemption, remains holy. Positional sanctification applies to our completed standing in Heaven. The moment a person is saved, he becomes a "new creature." – II Cor. 5:17

b. _Progressive_ sanctification. This is called experiential or practical sanctification and it takes place in this present life.

c. _Prospective_ sanctification. This is consummational sanctification, for God will not complete the process until we arrive in heaven. This is also called glorification.

4. _Personal_ separation. This separation is twofold. Holiness requires not only separation from sin, but also separation to God.

5. The basis for separation from sin. A questionable action or attitude is wrong if:

(1) It goes against the clear teaching of _Scripture_.

(2) It violates the _purity_ of mind.

(3) It produces impure thoughts or _actions_ – Matt. 5:28; II Cor. 11:3

(4) It is a _stumbling block_ to others. – I Cor. 8:8-13

(5) It is contrary to the _example of Christ_. – I Peter 2:21

(6) It offends the _conscience_. – James 4:17

(7) It will harm _one's walk_ with Christ. – II Cor. 6:14-17

(8) It will harm a believer's _body_. – I Cor. 6:18-20

(9) It will hurt _his faith_. – Rom. 14:23

Chapter Fourteen
Types of Christian Experiences[1]

"Christians' postconversion experiences vary. How can we classify the basic types of experiences, and what do they mean? How do they relate to a Christian's faith or doubts? What kind of outlook on signs and wonders reflects faith?" (13)

Conversion involves three time sequences:

1. _____ – includes the conviction of the Holy Spirit, desire, seeking, etc.

2. _____ – repentance, praying, regenerating, happiness, etc.

3. _____ – joy of Christ, relief from guilt, peace from tumult, confidence, etc.

Victory in the Christian life comes through the _____.

The purpose of this chapter is to summarize the various postconversion experiences that are prevalent through Christianity in order to help classify these experiences. Based on an analysis of experiences, the student should then be able to determine which experiences are biblical and reliable, and which experiences are fraudulent.

The following chart outlines the various categories of Christian Experiences:

Categories of Christian Experiences
EX – 1 Doctrinal Experience
EX – 1a Non-supernatural Experience
EX – 1b Orthodox Experience
EX – 2 The Deeper-life Experience
EX – 2a Christological Deeper-life Experience
EX – 2b Holy Spirit Deeper-life Experience
EX – 2c Soteriological Deeper-life Experience
EX – 3 Revival
EX – 4 Experiential Power for Service of Life
EX – 5 Victorious Experience
EX – 6 Sinless Experience
EX – 7 Intuitive Communication with God
EX – 8 Absorption Mystics
EX – 8a Trances, Visions, or Hearing Voices
EX – 8b Physical Manifestations
EX – 8c Asceticism

---

[1] *Understanding the Deeper Life,* (Old Tappan, NJ: Fleming H. Revell Company, 1988).

Some considerations and guidelines for Christian Experiences:

1. At times, different denominations and theological schools will explain the same working of the Holy Spirit within the lives of believers with _____ _____.

2. The list of 8 experiences measures the _____, not the spirituality of the experience. For example, "EX – 1 is objective Christianity, with a complete rejection of any forms of mysticism. EX – 8 is the ultimate mystical experience in which, according to the claims of mystics, the person is absorbed into God and loses his identity in the divine." (17)

3. Christians may experience some elements of each of the categories, but generally only one category will _____.

4. The believer will experience different categories at _____ _____.

5. People with similar needs and experiences will _____ _____.

6. There is a correlation between _____.

7. Some believers may, throughout the course of their lives, experience all 8 categories of Christian Experience.

8. Some believers may only experience _____ Christian Experiences their entire life.

9. When we get the Holy Spirit (at salvation), we get all of the Holy Spirit. As we "work out our salvation," we gradually give more of ourselves to the Holy Spirit. To teach that more of the Holy Spirit is necessary for effective ministry and continued sanctification is to _____.

EX – 1: Doctrinal Experience

The EX – 1 Doctrinal Experience can be divided into two distinct subcategories:
1. Those who _____ the supernatural
2. Those who _____ the supernatural

EX – 1 Doctrinal Experience
EX – 1a Non-supernatural Experience
EX – 1b Orthodox Experience

EX – 1a Non-supernatural Experience

1. John A. T. Robinson – wrote the book "Honest to God."
   a. did not feel the _____ in His life.
   b. book became the basis for the death of God movement.
2. Christian groups which deny the verbal-plenary inspiration of the Bible.
   a. deny the _____.
   b. do not expect or claim a _____.

> "So then for me the supreme truth of Christianity is that in Jesus I see God. When I see Jesus feeding the hungry, comforting the sorrowing, befriending men and women with whom no one else would have anything to do, I can say: 'This is God.' It is not that Jesus is God . . . But in Jesus I see perfectly and completely and finally, and once for all revealed and demonstrated, the attitude of God to men, the attitude of God to me." – William Barclay

The individual is committed to the lifestyle of the Ten Commandments, but denies the historic fundamentals of Christianity and the modern experience of a personal God living within the life of man.

EX – 1b Orthodox Experience

1. The individual accepts the historical accounts of miracles, but denies the presence of miracles in _____.
2. They believe the day of miracles is past but will one day reoccur when Christ returns.
3. Not to be confused with deists, who deny the total involvement of God with His creation.
4. The individual does not expect, or act upon the promises of the deeper Christian life.

Theology of the EX – 1 Experience:

1. "Their Christian experiences are probably just as _____ to them as any other experience." (17)
2. "Their experience is not directly from God to their hearts _____, from God, through the Bible, to them. God uses the means of His Word to produce an experience." (17)

EX – 2: The Deeper Christian Life

The Ex – 2 Experience takes the leap from objective doctrinal Christianity to the joy-filled, _____. The Spirit-led believer overcomes temptation and enjoys the presence of God in his daily life.

EX – 2 is available to Christians who:
1. _____.
2. Identify with Christ.
3. Recognize Christ's indwelling.
4. _____ the principles of Christian living from Scripture.
5. Express faith.
6. _____ in Christ.

I Corinthians 2:14-3:4 speaks of fleshly Christians, who have not overcome the tendencies of immaturity and spiritual shallowness prevalent within the Christian faith.

The Deeper Christian Life is also known as the following: _____, the victorious life, the crucified _____, the abundant life, the overcoming life, and the life of _____.

EX – 2 allows the Christian to:
1. Realize Jesus Christ dwells within them. 2. Enjoy positive emotions of love, joy, and peace. 3. _____. 4. Constantly control their lives and grow in grace. 5. Be _____ of salvation and guidance. 6. Have communion with God. 7. Obey the commands of Scripture regarding _____.

There are basically three subcategories within the EX – 2 Deeper-Life Experience:
1. Those who center their experience on _____.
2. Those who center their experience on the work of the _____ in their lives.
3. Those who center their experience on the aspect of the _____ _____.

EX – 2 Deeper-Life Experience
EX – 2a Christ-centered deeper life EX – 2b Holy Spirit-centered deeper life EX – 2c Cross-centered deeper life

Theology of the EX – 2: Deeper-Life Experience:
1. Experience is not based on one's _____.
2. The Christian does not _____ of self, his personality, limitations, or sinful tendencies.
3. The individual _____ with sin, temptation, and personal failures.
4. The Christian has learned the balance of living in _____ (the physical and the spiritual).

EX – 3: Revival

Definition of Revival: Revival is the outpouring of God upon His people. Some considerations when dealing with Revival:

1. What is man's part and what is God's part?
2. What stems from the individual's theology?
3. Revival is not a normal experience, but comes in certain seasons. _____.

How to recognize genuine Revival:
1. _____. What is the foundation of the experience?
2. _____. Where is the individual pointing . . . towards God or Himself?
3. Does it affect the _____?
   a. intellect, emotions, will
   b. speech, conduct, attitude, etc.
4. Does it affect _____?

EX – 4: Experiential Power

"Experiential power is more than the EX – 2 indwelling strength that the believer gets from Jesus Christ as he lives a deeper Christian life. One is from a person, the other power seems inherent in a system, and when the believer plugs into it, like plugging a toaster into an outlet, the power will flow." (30) The focus of this experience is _____ _____, including signs, wonders, casting out demons, raising the dead, but especially miraculous healings.

It is implied by Pat Robinson in his book, *The Secret Kingdom*, that an EX – 4 is almost as if the individual is surrounded by an invisible "bubble" world that is charged with spiritual power.

Theology of the EX – 4 experience:
1. Though it could be thought of as Pentecostalism, EX – 4 is not necessarily a _____.
2. Tied to the "_____" (referred to as the *baptism of the Holy Spirit* by some)
3. "It is _____ that is tied to their unique view of baptism of the Holy Spirit for exceptional service that is more than the filling of the Spirit (EX – 2) for a personal walk with God." (31,32)
4. "It is either ignorance of the plain requirements of God's word of the most daring presumption on our part when we try to do work for Christ until we know we have been Baptized with the Holy Spirit." – R. A. Torrey

EX – 5 Victorious Experience

Both the EX – 5 and EX – 6 experiences claim a _____, but the distinguishing feature is the potential to sin in the individual. The EX – 6 experience teaches the eradication of the sin nature, making the believer "_____," whereas the EX – 5 experience explains the believer as being "_____."

This experience, known as _____, includes the following elements:
1. The believer _____.
2. The believer being able not to sin.
3. The individual being _____.
4. The individual having new power from the Holy Spirit, _____.

This is an experience spanning holiness theology (Wesleyan, Methodist, Church of God, Anderson) and Pentecostal theology, which claim the experience is conjunction with the "_____."

EX – 6: Sinless Experience

"Some Christians claim they have had an experience after salvation in which their sinful nature is _____ or they gain a level of spirituality so that they _____ _____. Most say they no longer desire sin and they no longer actually sin." (34)

This involves a "_____:"
1. _____.
2. Searching his soul for sin.
3. Making _____ to God.
4. _____ until he experiences it.
5. Exercising _____ to secure the experience.

Theology of the EX – 6 experience:
1. Can include Pentecostal and non-Pentecostal theologies.
2. Certain Wesleyan groups claim to have the ability to live a perfect life, without the _____.
3. Certain Pentecostal theologies have concluded that the EX – 6 experience is _____, such as speaking in tongues, being slain in the Spirit, miracles, the gift of revelation, and other outward manifestations.

"EX – 6 practices may actually be EX – 2 deeper-life experience walks with God." (35, 36) Those claiming an EX – 6 experience may be deceived themselves or attempting to deceive others.

EX – 7: Intuitive Communication with God

Those experiencing EX – 7 experiences claim to have been in _____ _____. This extends beyond the believer's communication with God through prayer and the Scriptures, to the audible voice of God, or visions of God. The individual claims to have received a message from God that is more than just an _____.

Theology of the EX – 7 experience:

1. The EX – 7 experience is not confined to _____.
2. _____ can be found among Roman Catholics, Protestants, and cults.
3. There are _____ of communication with God.
4. The EX – 7 is distinguished from the EX – 4 in the _____ of the message.
5. Many would reject the EX – 7 experience, believing that revelation from God was completed with the closing of the _____.
6. The believer may be seen as having an EX – 4 experience (receiving a "word of knowledge"), but not a _____ (EX – 7).
7. If Scripture is seen as the _____, the EX – 7 experience does not have a place in the Christian life.

EX – 8: Absorption Mystics

"Some claim the ultimate experience of being united with God in the spirit or flesh so that they lose their _____." (37)

They lose sight of God being the "_____". They have confused the "_____.

Those claiming an EX – 8 experience have misplaced their sincerity, and it is _____ _____ as to their influence on God and His pleasure with them.

The EX – 8: Absorption Mystics contains three subcategories:

EX – 8: Absorption Mystics
EX – 8a Trances, visions, hearing voices EX – 8b Physical manifestations EX – 8c Asceticism

1. _____.
   a. Beyond the EX – 7 experience, to where the individual gives up control of their life, and _____ on visions or miraculous feats.
2. _____.
   a. Includes elements such as the _____ (the appearance of the wounds of Christ on an individual).
3. _____.
   a. Seeks to control their spiritual life by _____.
   b. Incorrect view of "beating my flesh," as used by Paul.

Chapter Fifteen
Types of Signs and Wonders

Introduction

"For every truth in life, there is a ___substitude___. For the reality of a deeper walk with Christ, there is a ___pseudoexperience___. One must always test the experience against Scripture." (56)

> Do you believe this statement? "Something is missing in your spiritual life if you have received the Holy Spirit yet have not spoken in tongues." – Dan Bashan

Signs that some claim evidence spirituality:
1. ___speaking in Tongues___.
2. Shouting.
3. Snake handling.
4. Performing ___miracles___.
5. Healings
6. Drinking poison.
7. ___Slain in the spirit___.
8. ___prophecy___.
9. Stigmata.
10. Raising the dead.

Just because a particular religious denomination or sect would practice one of the items listed above, does not mean that they would agree with all of them. In this chapter you will find an attempt to classify the various types of signs and wonders in order to better understand them.

> ### Manifestations
> Outward signs and wonders are physical manifestations of something working on the inside of the person. Most of the time the manifestation is because God is working in the person's heart. Because God is infinite and the person is finite, they can't contain God, so they express the inner work of God with their outer manifestation. I do not say God has given them outer manifestations. They are the person's work that expresses God's inner work. – Elmer Towns

Various opinions are prevalent concerning the origins of the contemporary Pentecostal movement:
1. _____ at the Bethel Bible Institute in Topeka, Kansas – December 31, 1900.
2. _____ reaching back to the apostolic era.

3. Full Gospel Business Men's Fellowship International and _____ – 1950s.

> "The Baptism of believers in the Holy Ghost is witnessed by the initial physical sign of speaking with other tongues . . ." – Statement of Fundamental Truths of the Assemblies of God (Article Eight)

> "We believe in the gift of tongues, prophecy, revelation, visions, healing, interpretations of tongues, etc." – Joseph Smith (Founder of the Mormons)

Categories of Signs and Wonders

"We believe there is a reality in the deeper Christian life that is more than the experience that grows out of _____ with Christianity." (60)

> ". . . and you in Me, and I in you." – John 14:20

Those who experience the presence of Christ know the reality of the deeper life, just as those who jump in a river know they are wet. The following categories are not designed to be hierarchical, but represent different expressions of miracles or the supernatural.

> ### CATEGORIES OF SIGNS AND WONDERS
>
> SW – 1: Biblical Miracles
> SW – 2: Counterfeit Miracles
> SW – 3: Psychosomatic Miracles
> SW – 4: Holistic-healing Miracles
> SW – 5: Confession-oriented Miracles
> SW – 6: Stimulated Miracles
> SW – 7: Pseudo Miracles
> SW – 8: Deceptive Miracles

Considerations:
1. The following categories recognize that every reported phenomenon _____ _____, and every genuine case may not necessarily be a direct act of God.
2. At times, God works directly by giving or providing a _____ to answer prayer.
3. These categories do not have _____ to any specific situations.

SW – 1: Biblical Miracles

Theology of Biblical Miracles:
1. These miracles find their origin in the __power of God__.
2. Similar to the miracles of the __prophets and apostles__.
3. If God answers prayer according to __His Word.__, then it is conceivable He will answer the prayer of faith with a miraculous healing.
4. This healing could be through the use of a doctor, medicine, etc., and would be an answer to the same prayer of faith.
5. Principles concerning the __possibility of miracles__ (George W. Peters):
   a. Since the gospel is supernatural in nature, it can also be in __manifestations__.
   b. It is a possibility that such miracle manifestations are a reenactment of the miracles of the __book of Acts__.
   c. It is important to make a distinction between miracles that relate to __man__ and those that relate to __nature__.
   d. When evaluating miracles, the Christian should remain __sober and vigilant__ but also __open and humble__.

SW – 2: Counterfeit Miracles

Theology of Counterfeit Miracles:
1. These are genuine miracles, but they have their origin __outside of God.__.
2. This type of miracle recognizes __the ministry of Satan__ as "…and angel of light." – II Corinthians 11:14
3. At times, Satan can work through individuals who use biblical __phraseology__ and claim they are having an evangelical experience.
4. By using the criteria of __Moses__ – Deuteronomy 18:20-22; 13:1-5, an individual can determine the credibility of a miracle. As the text instructs, a miracle from God will:
   a. be in the __Lord's name__. – 18:22
   b. not recognize __false gods__. – 13:2, 3
   c. __stimulate__ love for the Lord. – 13:3
   d. _____ with the Word of God – 13:4

SW – 3: Psychosomatic Miracles

Psychosomatic miracles can be defined as the __power of the mind__ over the body.

Theology of Psychosomatic Miracles:
1. There is an ever-increasing awareness "of the ability of the mind (*psyche*) to produce varied disturbances in the body (*soma*), hence the term *psychosomatic*." –S. I. McMillen
2. There is a need to distinguish between __faith healing__ and __devine healing__.

Divine healing comes through the gracious intervention of God.

3. A Divine healing could include the following:
    a. with or without medication.
    b. _Suddenly or gradually_ .
4. A "psychosomatic" healing would include:
    a. rests mainly on the individual's make-up and _____.
    b. principally a matter of _psychology and suggestions_ _____.
    c. little to do with divine intervention or the Gospel.
5. One who is healed psychosomatically is _actually healed._ , not in a
    SW – 1 (Biblical Miracle) fashion, but SW – 3 (Psychosomatic Miracle).

SW – 4: Holistic Healing Miracles

The body will _heal it itself_ if given the opportunity.

Theology of Holistic Healing Miracles:
1. "The fundamental premise of holistic healing is that the body can and will heal itself of some disease when positive mental health and corrective action are taken on the part of the sick." (64)
2. The individual must have a _positive mental attitude_ _____.
3. The nature of conversion is that a _radical change in lifestyle_ _____ can result in, among other things, a change in one's diet, resulting in health benefits to the new convert.
4. ". . . finding _____" (Carl Jung), can help change an individual's problems.

SW – 5: Confession-Oriented Miracles

Theology of Confession-Oriented Miracles:
1. Though classified as a miracle, this is actually a _____.
    A person must confess a healing in order to get healed.
2. This event can occur when an individual feels pressured into _____
    _____ that a miraculous event has occurred in their life.
3. This is further complicated in those situations where the desired miracle carries with it benefits such as _____ or acceptance into a particular group.
4. At times a believer may claim something in order _____
    in his or her own life, often times the individual claims something he doesn't have so he can get it.
5. The believer can actually "_____" a healing, when a healing has not occurred, and consequently die or suffer from the seriousness of the illness.

SW – 6: Stimulated Miracles

Theology of Stimulated Miracles:
1. Like confession-oriented miracles, stimulated miracles are actually _____ *non-miraculous events* .
2. They are a result of a ___*physical or psychological stimulus*___, such as music, hypnosis, or brainwashing.
3. Things such as drugs, physical posture, behavior, and special diets can also affect religious experiences, which in turn affect _____ .

SW – 7: Pseudo Miracles

Theology of Pseudo Miracles:
1. A pseudo miracle is promoted not for ulterior motives but largely *out of ignorance* involved in the reported sign and wonder.
2. The ___*Indonesian Revival*___ (1960) reported raising the dead, which forced many to examine the issue of pseudo miracles.
   a. There are different ways of explaining when someone is considered "dead:"
      1) heart stops beating
      2) no brain activity
      3) no breath to lungs
      4) a coma
   b. A better explanation for the actual event is not resurrection, but rather, ___*resuscitation.*___ .

> "According to my concept of death, *no search such miracles happens* I learned again the value of seeing words and concepts from the people's point of view and interpreting them according to their mentality and understanding." – George Peters

SW – 8: Deceptive Miracles

Theology of Deceptive Miracles:
1. Some alleged signs and wonders that have been *humanly faked or deceptively reported* .
2. One must first determine the ___*authenticity*___ of the miracles, and then the ___*motive*___ behind the miracle must be accounted for.

DISCERNING THE AUTHORITY OF MIRACLE WORKERS

> "The presence of the above eight types of signs and wonders in the contemporary evangelical experience only serves to stress the need to exercise spiritual discernment in evaluating alleged miracles and those who are chiefly involved in their performance." (68)

According to George Peters, there are four types of miracles that are nearly universally accepted by Christians:

1. Healings which are primarily __psychological__. (You were never sick, but you thought you were healed).
2. Psychological healing and restoration as a result of the __experience of salvation__.
3. __Liberation__ from demonic influences, powers, and direct demon-possession, as a result of salvation.
4. Direct divine intervention, which brings __healing__ and __restoration__ of the body.

The need for discernment when considering miraculous experiences is evidenced in both Jewish history and the church. The following is a list of seventeen characteristics of the true servant of God in speaking in the prophetic office:

1. _____ in the name of the Lord. – Deuteronomy 18:22
2. _____ shall come to pass. – Deuteronomy 18:22
3. Does not advocate the worship of false gods. – Deuteronomy 13:2,3
4. Promotes _____ for the Lord. – Deuteronomy 13:3
5. Life and teaching consistent with the _____. – Deuteronomy 13:4
6. Promotes _____ in the Lord. – Deuteronomy 13:4
7. Teaching is not characterized by perverseness, _____.
   – Jeremiah 23:25-34; Acts 20:30
8. Produces _____ characteristic of the servant of the Lord.
   – Matthew 7:15-20
9. Has a _____ of God.
   – Matthew 7:21-23
10. Does not attempt to raise _____ but rather
    to the Lord. – Acts 20:30
11. Ministry not characterized by _____.
    – II Peter 2:1; I John 4:2,3
12. Adheres to _____ of the evangelical faith.
    – II Peter 2:1; I John 4:2,3
13. Concerned with _____ rather than using others to attain personal goals. – II Peter 2:3
14. Practices _____ to God from the world. – I John 3:6
15. Remains loyal to the _____ rather that a more contemporary or "advanced" teaching. – II John 9,10
16. Promotes a _____ as a consistent response to biblical doctrine. – Jude 4
17. Has a proper respect for _____. – Jude 8

> The refusal of a religious leader to repent of known sin or error is specifically identified by the Lord as characteristic of the false teacher. – Revelation 2:21

BIBLICAL TEACHINGS REGARDING SIGNS AND WONDERS

What is a miracle?

> A miracle is the _____ of nature by God. – C. S. Lewis

1. "Something that _____"
2. All healing is _____, even if it involves medical treatment. – Kathryn Kuhlman
3. "A miracle has been generally defined to be a _____, setting aside, or suspending, the laws of nature." – Charles Grandison Finney
4. "A miracle is an event in nature, so extraordinary in itself and so coinciding with the prophecy or command of a religious teacher or leader, as to fully warrant the conviction, on the part of those who witness it, that God has wrought it with the design of certifying that this teacher or leader has been _____." – Augustus Hopkins Strong
5. "A genuine miracle is an unusual event, accomplishing some useful work, and revealing the _____ of God." – Henry Thiessen
6. "A miracle is a _____ resulting from divine interposition" – George W. Peters

Five Greek Words for Miracles
1. *terata*: "_____"
2. *erga*: "_____"
3. *thaumasin*: "_____"
4. *dunameis*: "_____"
5. *semeion*: "_____"

> "A miracle is a spectacular (*terata*) thing (*thaumasin*) or work (*erga*) expressing the power of God (*dunameis*) for some signal purpose (*semeion*)."

The Theology of Signs and Wonders:
1. "The debate over whether miracles can happen today centers around one's understanding of _____."
2. A sign usually points to the message from God and gives the message _____.
3. According to W. E. Vines, the use of the term "_____" in Scripture can mean three different things:
   a. "that which distinguished a person of God from others."
      1) Matt. 26:48; Luke 2:12; Rom. 4:11
   b. "_____"
      1) Matt. 12:29; Luke 2:34
   c. "_____"
      1) tokens of divine authority and power – Matt. 12:38,39; John 2:11
      2) by demons – Rev. 16:14
      3) by false teachers or prophets – Matt 24:24; Mark 13:22

4) by Satan through his special agents – II Thess. 2:9; Rev. 13:13
5) of tokens portending future events – Matt. 24:3; Mark 13:4; Rev. 12:1

> Signs confirming of what God had accomplished in the atoning sacrifice of Christ, His resurrection and ascension, and of the sending of the Holy Spirit, were given to the Jews for their recognition, as at Pentecost, and supernatural operations in the churches, such as the gift of tongues and prophesying; there is no record of the continuance of these latter after the circumstances recorded in Acts 19:1-20. – W. E. Vines

Eight Reasons why the gift of tongues has ceased:
1. _____ never spoke in tongues, nor predicted them (argument from silence).
2. _____ to speak in tongues (they are descriptive not prescriptive).
3. _____ in Bible.
    a. _____, i.e., Day of Pentecost. "How hear we every man in his own tongue" – Acts 2:8
    b. _____, i.e., "Though I speak with the tongues of men and of angels" – I Cor. 13:1. This is God's language that was corrupted at the Tower of Babel.
4. The purpose of a sign was to give credibility to the message of God and the establishment of New Testament truth. "Wherefore, tongues are for a sign" – I Cor. 14:22. The spiritual gift of tongues and the interpretation of tongues have passed.
5. If we can prove one "spiritual gift" _____, then there is foundation to believe tongues have ceased, i.e., no more apostles who saw Jesus and walked with Jesus. – Acts 1:21-22
6. _____. Missionaries cannot use/have not used this gift when facing a new language.
7. Most of the _____ haven't spoken in tongues (argument of silence).
8. Former tongues speakers and present tongue speakers have confessed to _____ _____, i.e., pretending.

TODAY'S MIRACLES

It is evident that God works within His creation today. He is not an absentee God. The following is a breakdown of SW – 1: Biblical Miracles:
1. SW – 1a: _____ – The salvation of the individual
2. SW – 1b: _____ – illumination of the believer and supernatural guidance
3. SW – 1c: _____ – Peace of God, Joy, Love, fruit of the Spirit and conviction and guilt of sin
4. SW – 1d: _____ – the believer is led by God into the Will of God
5. SW – 1e: _____ – redirection of circumstances, control of situations, or interference

6. SW – 1f: _____ – Filling of the Spirit, the indwelling Christ, and victory over sin
7. SW – 1g: _____ – the eradication of the old nature; the power of the Holy Spirit; signs and wonders; the ability to refrain from sin; baptism of the Holy Spirit
8. SW – 1h: _____ – raising the dead; the Ascension; parting of the Red Sea.
9. SW – 1i: _____ – Creation; incarnation; inspiration of Scripture – these are the bases of the deeper Christian life.

> Miracles are a possibility whenever and wherever the power of the Gospel breaks through in new ways and places. The New Testament does not explicitly close the door on such possibilities. We have no right to deny they happen today, nor to expect and demand them. The Bible remains silent and open in this matter. It should not surprise us, however, if miracles do accompany the introduction of the Gospel in new areas and among people held in bondage by occultism, spiritism, and demonism." – George W. Peters (Dallas Theological Seminary)

Chapter Sixteen
Living in Two Worlds

> " . . . you in Me, and I in you . . ." – John 14:20
> " . . . abide in Me, and I in you . . ." – John 15:4

INTRODUCTION

To understand the deeper Christian life, one must understand the concept of living in two worlds. This principle can be summarized by using various terms:

1. _Union and communion_.
2. _Salvation and sanctification_.
3. The believer's _State_ and _Standing_.

The believer is united with Christ in _at Salvation_ (union), and then the believer grows in Christ in _Sanctification_ (communion).

The Standing and State of a Christian:

Much confusion has resulted from a misunderstanding of the distinction between a believer's _standing before God_, and one's _State on the earth_. The deeper-life Christian must learn to live in two worlds at the same time. Having been clothed with Christ's righteousness, the believer has a perfect standing before God in heaven, yet that same believer still struggles with sin. As Paul states in I Timothy 1:15, " . . . Christ Jesus came into the world to save sinners; of whom I am chief." The promise of Jesus Christ to indwell the believer enables him to be guided and encouraged, but the battle with sin remains – I John 1:8. The following chart visualizes this distinction:

Standing before God

State on earth

Unsaved Man   Salvation

Standing before God	State on earth
Non - experiential *Perfect in Christ* No separation from God *Joy and peace* *Justified* *No broken relationship*	Experiential Sinner in practice *Fellowship can be broken* Heartache and disappointment *Temptations and trials* *Broken fellowship*

This chapter is designed to explain the believer's standing before God in heaven. Three words / phrases (involving five Greek terms), which help to explain the believer's perfection in Christ, will be used to help further explain this principle. They are, "___*together*___" (Greek words *meta* and *sun*), "___*partnership*___" (Greek words *metochos* and *koinonos*), and "___*in Christ*___" (Greek word *en Christo*).

> "The majority of Christians much more frequently think of Christ as a Savior outside of them, than as a Savior who dwells within. This comparative neglect of the doctrine is doubtless a reaction from the exaggerations of a false mysticism. But there is great need of rescuing the doctrine from neglect. . . . The doctrine of Union with Christ, in like manner, is taught so variously and abundantly, that to deny it is to deny inspiration itself." – Augustus Hopkins Strong

TOGETHER WITH CHRIST

What is the doctrine of togetherness with Christ?
1. To doctrine of "togetherness" teaches that the believer has been ___*crucified with Christ*___ _____. – Romans 6:6; Galatians 2:20
2. Paul uses the term *sun* to indicate the fact that the believer is one with Christ in heaven, or ___*together with Christ*___.
3. Many misunderstand the doctrine of togetherness; they want to turn a ___*past*___ non-experiential truth into a ___*present*___ experience.
4. "The position of ___*Christ*___ defines the position of the ___*Christian*___." – C. H. M.
5. The deeper-life emphasis will not make a believer think he is perfect that drives him into mysticism, but rather makes him realize he is ___*responsible*___ to bring his earthly life into conformity with this heavenly life.

THE TOGETHERNESS OF THE BELIEVER AND CHRIST

1. United together	Romans 6:5
2. Hidden with Christ in God	Colossians 3:3
3. _crucified with Christ_	Romans 6:6; Galatians 2:20
4. Died with Christ	Colossians 2:20
5. _Buried with Christ_	Colossians 2:12; Romans 6:4
6. Made us alive together with Christ	Ephesians 2:5; Colossians 2:13
7. _Raised up together (with Christ)_	Ephesians 2:6; Colossians 2:12; 3:31
8. Made us sit together	Ephesians 2:6
9. To be _conformed together_	Romans 8:29; Philippians 3:20,21
10. Fellow workers, workers together	I Corinthians 3:9; II Corinthians 6:1
11. We _suffer with Him_	Romans 8:17
12. Joint heirs with Christ	Romans 8:17
13. _Glorified_ together	
14. We shall live together	Romans 6:8; II Timothy 2:11; I Thessalonians 5:10
15. We shall _reign with Him_	II Timothy 2:12

What is meant by the phrase " _Crucified with Christ_ **"?**
1. The believer's union with Christ begins _at conversion_ and matures through the observance of the Lord's Supper – Archibald Hodge
2. Some feel they must "crucify" the _old-self_ before the new man can give them the _abundant life_ .
   a. "Life-giving preaching costs the preacher much – death to self, crucifixion to the world, the travail of his own soul. Crucified preaching only can give life. Crucified preaching can come only from a crucified man." – E. M. Bounds
   b. "In every Christian's heart there is a cross and a throne, and the Christian is on the throne till he puts himself on the cross; if he refuses the cross he remains on the throne . . . We want to be saved but we insist that Christ do all the dying."
3. Those who reject the _post-conversion crucifixion_ of self do so on the two theological arguments:
   a. The post-conversion crucifixion implies an _active role_ on the part of the believer.
   b. Paul describes co-crucifixion in terms of a _conversion-related experience_ . – Galatians 2:20; Romans 6:4

"So also in historical fact we can say, reverently but with equal accuracy, 'I was crucified when Christ was crucified,' or 'Christ was crucified when I was crucified,' for they are not two historical events, but one. My crucifixion was with Him . . . . Praise the Lord, when He died on the Cross I died with Him." – Watchman Nee

When was the believer co-crucified with Christ?

1. On the day of ___preparation___ (AD 30).
2. " . . . the Lamb slain from the ___foundation of the world___ " – Revelation 13:8
3. On the ___first Christian Pentecost___ – I Corinthians 12:13; Acts 2:1-4
4. Personal ___conversion___ – Galatians 2:20
5. Personal ___baptism___ – Romans 6:4

WHEN IS THE BELIEVER CRUCIFIED TOGETHER WITH CHRIST?	
Theological Perspective	Before the foundation of the world – Revelation 13:8
Historical Perspective	Historically on Golgotha when Christ was crucified – Matthew 27:35
Ecclesiastic Perspective	At the first Christian Pentecost – I Corinthians 12:13; Acts 2:1-4
Soteriological Perspective	At the moment of the individual's conversion – Galatians 2:20
Testimonial Perspective	At the believer's baptism – Romans 6:4
Experiential Perspective	In the practicing of reckoning myself dead to sin – Romans 6:11

Principles Concerning a Believer's "___Togetherness with Christ___":
From a broad perspective, it is apparent that a believer's union with Christ is a ___conversion ~~to~~ related experience___.

1. As a believer better understands his conversion experience, he will feel as though he is being drawn ___close to Christ___.
2. There is often a ___delay in time___ from conversion until the time when the believer realizes and appreciates his position in Christ.
3. The Bible makes it clear that the believer could not become closer to God than he is when he accepts Christ. From the very beginning, he is close to God because of his ___standing before God in heaven___.
4. The difference between the Keswick Christian and other evangelicals is not so much his deeper experience with Christ as it is his ___deeper understanding and application___ of a common experience.
5. At times it is difficult to understand the distinction between a believer's ___standing___ before God and his ___state___ on earth.
6. Perhaps the most complete statement of the nature of the union of the believer and Christ is the expression offered by Paul, "For we have been untied together in the likeness of His death." – Romans 6:5

> I have been crucified with Christ [standing]; it is no longer I who live, but Christ lives in me [state] . . ." – Galatians 2:20

PARTNERSHIP WITH CHRIST

The concept of the believer's partaking of the nature of Christ is clearly stated in Scripture on two occasions:

1. *metochos* – " <u>partakers</u> " – twice used in an argument emphasizing the chastening of God as an evidence of true sonship
   - " . . . that we may be partakers of His holiness." – Hebrew 12:10
2. *koinonos* – " <u>partakers</u> " – used by Peter in the context of the promises of God
   - " . . . that through these you may be partakers of the divine nature . . ." – II Peter 1:4

What can be learned from these terms?

1. It should be noted that both of these terms were <u>commercial expressions</u> describing a business partnership in Greek culture.
2. These terms are used throughout the Gospels to refer to the <u>fishing business</u> involving Peter, Andrew, James and John.
3. According to A. T. Robertson, *metochos* carries with it the connotation of "participation with one in <u>common blessings</u> – Heb. 3:1,14; 6:4; 12:8," while *koinonos* "has the notion of <u>personal fellowship.</u>, partnership."
4. Note in the relationship the believer <u>does not lose his identity</u>, nor is he <u>absorbed into God</u>. He is in union with God (<u>non - experiential</u>) but not absorbed into God so that he loses his personality.

> "It cannot be taken in so literal a sense as to mean that we can even partake of the divine *essence*, or that we shall be *absorbed* into the divine nature so as to lose our individuality . . ." – Albert Barnes commenting on II Peter 1:4

"Partnership with Christ" and Mysticism

1. Those who teach a <u>co - nature</u> with Christ would teach that a believer must yield himself to Christ so that he loses his <u>self - identity</u> or his own personality in God.

> "The force of the preposition *sun*, as added to the adjective would be much that of co-, '*associated with, made participants of this or that*, etc. – "*made of one nature*,' co-natured." – Early Brethren view

2. It should be kept in mind that there is always an " <u>I – Thou</u> " relationship between the Christian and God.
3. Since God indwells the believer, he should allow God to work through him for new <u>power</u> and new <u>motives</u>.
4. When the believer becomes a partaker of the divine nature, it means he has a moral nature that is born anew, not that he loses his <u>nature or identity</u>.

Pauline Illustrations of the Believer's Union with Christ:

1. A _building and its foundation_ – Ephesians 2:20-22

> ". . . having been built on the foundation of the apostles and prophets, Jesus Christ Himself being the chief cornerstone, in whom the whole building, being fitted together, grows into a holy temple in the Lord, in whom you also are being built together for a dwelling place of God in the Spirit." – Ephesians 2:20-22

   a. The believer has an attachment to Christ, the building's _cornerstone_.
   b. The cornerstone was the _governing piece_ for the entire building, determining how the rest of the building would be constructed.
   c. "Each one [Gentile and Jew] is a part of His house which is built upon the foundation of the apostles and prophets of the New Testament, secured by its corner-stone, that corner-stone which gives unity to all the superstructure which is rising from it . . ." – Earl D. Radmacher

2. Members of the _body and it head_ – I Corinthians 6:15; 12:12; Ephesians 1:22, 23

> "And He put all things under His feet, and gave Him to be head over all things to the church, which is His body, the fullness of Him who fills all in all." – Ephesians 1:22, 23

   a. The emphasis in this illustration is on _Christ as the head_ and individual believers as the members.
   b. A close connection between the believer and Christ is evidenced, while maintaining the _distinctiveness_.
   c. "As the Head of the Body, then, Christ is both _distinct from the body and inseparable_ from it. He unites the body in Himself, and is yet not to be identified with it . . . The Body lives only because it draws power from the head, but it is not identical with the Head." – J. Robert Nelson
   d. Christ is indisputably in control not only of the body but also of the individual members of that body.
   e. "I attribute the highest importance to the connection between the head and the members; to the inhabitation of Christ in our hearts; in a word, to the mystical union by which we enjoy him, so that, being made ours, he makes us partakers of the blessings with which he is furnished." – John Calvin

3. Relationship of a _husband and wife_ – Romans 7:4; Ephesians 5:31, 32

> "For this reason a man shall leave his father and mother and be joined to his wife, and the two shall become one flesh." This is a great mystery, but I speak concerning Christ and the church." – Ephesians 5:31, 32

a. This is the most intimate of the three concepts, for the Christian is pictured as the _bride of Christ_

b. The emphasis of this partnership illustration is not the distinctiveness of the partners, but rather their _attachment to each other_ .

c. The verb, *proskouma*, literally meaning "_glued together with_ ," is the strongest of the four Greek verbs which the New Testament identifies the attachments between two objects or two individuals.

d. It is interesting to note that the initiative and effort involved in this joining appears wholly on the part of _Christ_ .

> This fellowship in heaven is our association with Christ (our standing in heaven), which becomes the basis for participation of fellowship with Christ (our state on earth).

Alexander Archibald Hodge identifies several aspects of fellowship of the believer with Christ:

1. _____ with Christ in his covenant standings and rights.

2. _____ with Christ in the transforming, assimilating power of His life, making the Christian like Christ and leading to the Christian's victorious reaction to labors, sufferings, temptation, and death.

3. Christ has rightful fellowship with the Christian _____.

4. The believer holds fellowship with Christ in the spiritual reception of the

_____.

5. Being united with Christ, all believers have _____.

Principles Concerning a Believer's "_____"

1. The believer's individual fellowship with Christ is the _____ of his fellowship with others within the family of God.

2. What is true between individual members within the body is true _____ _____ between the member and the Head.

3. "Let us not forget that what we are is more important than what we do, and that all fruit borne when not abiding in Christ must be fruit of the flesh and not of the Spirit. As wounds when healed often leave a scar, so the sin of neglected communion may be forgiven and yet the effect remain permanently." – J. Hudson Taylor

4. "One of the heaviest problems in the Christian life is that of _____: how to become as pure as we know we ought to be and must be if we are to enjoy intimate communion with a holy God." – A. W. Tozer

5. The believer should not seek union; _____. As A. W. Tozer states, "If only we would stop lamenting and look up, God is here. Christ is risen."

6. Based on his [the believer's] union with Christ (standing), he can go deeper in _____ (state). Based on his salvation (standing in the heavenlies), he can get victory over sin (state). This is not sinless perfection, but the _____ of God's children.

7. The tendency within Christianity to identify some as "_____" Christians has no biblical basis, for all believers are equally united with Christ.

8. The _____ deeper life of the believer is possible because of his _____ standing in heaven.

> The deeper Christian life is possible. It is based on a believer's union with Christ. The believer is saved, justified, and is perfect before God in heaven (union with Christ or standing in heaven). Therefore, he must seek God in prayer, yield, and rid himself of sin (communion with Christ or state on earth).

Chapter Seventeen
The Believer's Position "in Christ"

INTRODUCTION

Union with Christ is taught by three truths. First the Greek words translated "_together_" (*sun* and *meta*) mean we have been placed with Christ in heaven. Second, the words translated as "_partakers_" (*metochos* or *koinonos*) mean we have the moral nature of Christ and have His life. Third, the words *en Christo*, "_in Christ_," describe the believer's position at salvation and throughout his Christian life. Having previously considered the believer's togetherness and partnership with Christ, attention will now be given to the Christian's position in Christ.

Questions Concerning the Christian's Position "in Christ":
1. Can one live in a state of sinless perfection?
2. Can one eradicate the sinful nature?
3. Can one eliminate the desire (lust) of sin?
4. Can someone claim to be without sin?
   a. some are _ignorant_.
   b. some are _deceive themselves_ of the definition of sin.
   c. some _____.

> Some think they are perfect because they only understand half the biblical expectations for Christians. The Bible seems to teach two extremes for the believer. First, the child of God is told to " . . . Be ye holy . . ." – I Peter 1:15 or "Be ye perfect – Matthew 5:48. On the other hand, Paul testified, "I am the chief of sinners" (I Timothy 1:15), and John stated, "If we say that we have no sin, we deceive ourselves . . ." – I John 1:8

The believer must learn to _____ theses two extremes as he lives out the Christian life. Though it is inaccurate to think that one can live , it is also incorrect to indulge in sin, enjoy sin, and make no effort to _____ _____.

Scriptural Teaching Concerning the Perfection of Believers:
1. Various concepts / phrases are used in Scripture to describe the Christian's position of perfection:
   a. "_in Christ_"
   b. "the believer's _standing_"
   c. "the believer's _union_"
   d. "_in the heavenlies_"
2. As with all doctrines, there is a tendency to misinterpret and misunderstanding this theme of Scripture. Though the believer's position in Christ is one of perfection, this is a _non-experiential perfection_.

3. When conversion is viewed as an ___experiential process___, it is only natural to interpret the phrase "in Christ," which relates to conversion, as ___experiential___.

4. A person's experience involves a total commitment of his ___total personality___, not merely to a religious philosophy or dogma, but to a person.

5. In the thirteen epistles that bear his name, Paul uses the expression "in Christ" ___172 times___.

6. The following chart highlights some of Paul's use of the term "in Christ":

Biblical Teaching of Paul:	Reference:
___NO Condemnation___ for those "in Christ"	Romans 8:1
Christian's are ___alive___ unto God "in Christ"	Romans 6:11
If any man is "in Christ" he is a ___new creature___	II Corinthians 5:17
Paul was ___crucified___ and Christ ___lived in me___	Galatians 2:20
We are _____ "into Christ"	Galatians 3:27
We are _____ "in Christ Jesus unto good works"	Ephesians 2:10

BEING "IN CHRIST"

There are several interpretations of the phrase "in Christ." A person's theological suppositions will determine how he interprets this truth.

Eight Interpretations of the phrase "in Christ"
1. Mystery-Religion Influence
2. Sacramental Orientation
3. A Meaningless Idiomatic Expression
4. The Republican View
5. A Metaphor for a Believer's Communion
6. Being in the Spirit of Christ
7. In the Universal Church
8. In the Person of Christ in the Heavenlies

ONE: Mystery-Religion Influence
1. Some writers tend to interpret Paul in terms of the ___pagan mystery religions___ common to his time.

2. The assumption is made that Paul _borrowed concepts_ or at least the language of these cults to express his own view of Christianity.
3. "Christianity has not borrowed from the mystery religions, because it was always, at least in Europe, a _____ itself." – Kirrsopp Lake
4. D. Miall Edwards limits the connection to simply _language_: "The characteristics which his [Paul's] teaching has in common with the pagan religions are simply a witness to the common religious wants of mankind, and not to his indebtedness to them."

TWO: Sacramental Orientation
1. Some who argue for the connection between Paul and Hellenistic mystery religion tend to interpret the expression "in Christ" _Sacramentally_ and view baptism and the Lord's Table as initiatory rites of Christianity.
2. "In primitive Christianity baptism guaranteed the forgiveness of sins and allegiance to the coming Messiah, and the prospect of sharing the glory which is to dawn at His coming . . . On this basis he asserts that what takes place in baptism is the beginning of the being-in-Christ and the process of dying and rising again which is associated therewith." – Albert Schweitzer
3. Perhaps a better understanding is the fact that, for Paul, baptism is not a means of grace effecting salvation but rather the _symbolic testimony_ to the reception of the grace that brings salvation (see I Corinthians 1:17).

THREE: A Meaningless Idiomatic Expression
1. Some attempt to deny any _significance_ of the phrase "in Christ."
2. "Strictly speaking, from an abstract point of view, it means nothing in itself; it always needs the appeal of particular circumstances to take shape and receive its extraordinary fullness." – Michel Bouttier
3. "It is clear that the expressions "in the Holy Spirit," "in Christ," and "in the Lord" become more frequent as the style becomes more _rhetorical_ and they tend to become _stylistic ornament_." – Lucien Cerfaux
4. The reasoning behind this view appears to be based on circular reasoning, for one can only conclude that Paul would use the term 172 times as a "
" only if one assumes it has no other significance.

FOUR: The Republican View
1. Those holding to a republican or representative view deny a _mystical union_ of Christ and believers.
2. This view tends to limit this concept to the act of _justification_, assuming the role of Christ as only the federal head of the race.
3. "It is a legal or _federal union_, so that all of our legal or covenant responsibilities rest upon Christ, and all his legal or covenant mercies accrue to us . . ." – Alexander Archibald Hodge

4. The difficulty with this view is not so much in what it states but in what it ___leaves unsaid___. It must be kept in mind that the believer is made a new creature "in Christ," which goes beyond the realm of justification – II Corinthians 5:17

5. While being in Christ involves the act of ___justification___, it also involves far more than a mere change in one's _legal standing_ before God.

FIVE: A Metaphor for a Believer's Communion

1. Historically, the ___Roman Catholic Church___ has tended to emphasize this view from a corporate perspective, that is, to be "in Christ" is to be part of the "holy catholic church."

2. ___Non – Catholic___ theologians are also beginning to consider this view. As Rudolph Bultmann states, "to belong to the Christ Church is to be 'in Christ' or 'in the Lord.'"

3. "The church is literally now the resurrection 'body' of Christ." – John A. T. Robinson

4. The fault in this view is not in what it states, but in what it ___leaves unsaid___. There can be no disputing that being "in Christ" is the basis for an intimate communion with Christ, both personally and corporately in the church, which is His body, but it cannot be limited to a mere metaphor of personal or corporate communion.

SIX: Being in the Spirit of Christ

1. *In Christ* means "a literal local dative of personal existence in the pneumatic Christ." – Adolph Deissmann

2. This view tends to take away from the ___personality___ of Jesus Christ.

3. " . . . as Jesus is reported to have spoken of His relationship to the Father as being "*in* the Father," all without diminishing the concept of the real personality of God, so Paul, with his high ___Christology___, can speak of being "in Christ" without that concept of person "in" person softening or dissolving the fixed outlines of personality for either Christ or the Christian." – Richard N. Longenecker

SEVEN: In the Universal Church

1. Some ___dispensationalists___ have used the phrase to mean the believer is placed into the body of Christ, which is the universal church.

2. "The expression "___in Christ___" in every one of its many instances in the New Testament refers to the saints of this dispensation." – John F. Walvoord

3. This action took place in the ___baptism of the Spirit___ – I Corinthians 12:13, and produces a non-experiential position for the believer.

EIGHT: In the Person of Christ in the Heavenlies

1. This view is similar to the one immediately above, but notes that the believer is placed into

_____*in the heavenlies*_____, not just a
heavenly church entity.

2. This relationship can be seen in the example of a _*pregnant woman*_.
   Both the mother and the child are _*distinct entities*_, yet even
   medical treatment for one will affect the other.

WHEN WAS THE BELIEVER PLACED "IN CHRIST"	
_____	On Golgotha
Positionally	Day of Pentecost
Actually	At his conversion
_____	At the believer's baptism

3. The believer being placed in Christ is only _____, for
   John 14:20 states, " . . . Ye in Me, and I in you."

4. The first is _____; the believer is positionally "in
   Christ." The second is _____ and is based on the first,
   "Christ in me."

Just because we say to be "in Christ" is non-experiential does not mean we do not have
a experience related to it. You cannot be "in Christ" without having "_____."
So when you experience Christ in your life, the experience is based on your being "in
Christ.

5. "We have in fact no way of getting in, but what is more important, we need not try
   to get in, for we *are* in. What we could not do for ourselves,
   _____. *He has put us into Christ.*" – Watchman Nee

6. The experience of being placed in Christ _____,
   whereas usually at some later point, the believer enters into or experiences the
   reality of this truth (some understand it at conversion).

Being "in Christ" is therefore a description of the believer not only at conversion but
also throughout his Christian experience. In identifying the believer's position "in
Christ," Paul also hints further at the intimacy that exists between the believer and his
Lord . . . This concept involves a greater degree of intimacy than may be implied in the
togetherness statements or partnership statements of Paul. The truth of "in Christ"
establishes a bridge between the believer's association with Christ and living in Christ.

Chapter Eighteen
Union and Communion

Introduction

Understanding the Terms:

1. Conversion is described with the phrase "_____."
2. Continuing fellowship with God is described with the phrase "_____
   _____."
3. These terms have also been called _____ (union with God) and
   _____ (communion with God).
4. Union with God is a _____ within the Christian's life;
   communion with God is something that _____.
5. There are elements of _____ within the doctrine of Communion
   with God, but these terms must be defined for correct understanding:

> Mysticism means communion with God, that is to say with a Being conceived as the supreme and ultimate reality. If what the mystics say of their experience is true, if they have really been in communion with the Holy Spirit of God, that is a fact of overwhelming importance, which must be taken into account when we attempt to understand God, the world, and ourselves. – W. R. Inge

6. Properly understood, union becomes the _____ for communion.
7. Though all Christians *experience* union with Christ, not all believers _____
   the communion with Christ that is available.

> The new birth makes us partakers of the divine nature. There the work of undoing the dissimilarity between us and God. . . . From there it progresses by the sanctifying operation of the Holy Spirit till God is satisfied. That is the theology of it, but as I said, even the unregenerate soul may sometimes suffer from the feeling that God is far from him. – A. W. Tozer

8. A mystic is by definition, anyone who enjoys any _____.
9. I tell everyone, "I am a mystic," but not like the Catholic mystics, I am a _____
   _____, because all my experience is based on the Bible.

Steps to Communion

Union with Christ is a _____ that is accomplished by God apart from any human effort or involvement. It comes from conversion. Union with Christ becomes the basis for a believer's communion with Christ, which is _____ within the believer's life.

There are usually six acts in the experience of the believer associated with entering into communion with Christ:

Step One: _____
1. For some, merely _____ of the believer's togetherness with Christ – his position in Christ and full union with Christ – is the beginning of a deeper communion with Christ.
2. One cannot fully appreciate truth he does not first at least partially understand _____.
3. Since _____ may or may not be a proper interpretation of communion, everyone needs a standard outside himself to determine the right approach to God.
4. _____ is the rule by which to judge all feelings.

Step Two: _____
1. The believer should repent of _____ in order to enter into deeper communion with God.
2. Other terms for *repentance* include:
    a. "_____"
    b. "_____"
    c. "_____"
3. The process of repentance:
    a. believer searches his heart _____ that blocks his fellowship with God
    b. believer sincerely seeks _____ for this sin
    c. believer asks God to forgive his sin by _____. – I John 1:7
    d. believer promises to _____ from the experience so it doesn't happen again.
4. Repentance involves more than just turning from the known sin within the believer's life. It must be accompanied by an awareness of the Christian's lack of _____ _____ of communion with God. The believer must realize that they do not always seek God in prayer, and they do not always try to walk by faith.

Step Three: _____
1. Faith is _____ in His Word.
2. Often times, entering into communion with Christ is a matter of _____ the Word of God.
3. The _____ of faith, which allows Christ to enter and live within the heart, must be extended into a _____ of faith in His Person, which allows Him to settle down and feel at home. – Stuart Briscoe
4. How does a believer enter the deeper-life of faith?
    a. the believer must _____ the Scriptural commands
    b. faith is _____ the Word of God to one's life so you know what the Bible teaches about living in the power of "Christ's love."
    c. believers must let Christ _____ so the power of Christ's faith can flow through them.

5. The deeper life of faith is the result of the believer's _____ to have communion with God.

Step Four: _____
1. "You have trusted Him to forgive and forget your past, and you expect Him to deliver you safely in heaven. Therefore, you *must* give Him the right to prove Himself to be as capable of organizing and directing in *time*, as you know and expect Him to be adequate for *eternity*." – Briscoe
2. When a person yields his life to God, it is more than _____. The believer takes control of his life by deciding to always _____.
3. Yielding to God is an _____; the believer knows what should not control his life (sin, temptation, harmful influence), and he knows that God desires and is able to control his life, so he _____.
4. Correct yielding is based on _____.
5. Yielding is a "neutral action" incorporated in various spiritual activities including:
   a. being _____.
   b. understanding the Scriptures (_____).
   c. _____ effectively.
   d. living by _____.
   e. being led by the Spirit.

> The action of yielding does not make you spiritual; the person to whom you yield (Christ) makes you spiritual. Christ is the measure of your spirituality.

Step Five: _____
1. The attitude of yielding must be continued through the act of _____.
2. "The consecration of all to our master, far from lessening our power to impact, increases both _____ in ministration." – J. Hudson Taylor

Step Six: _____
1. Some believe this is a second experience after salvation, in which God _____ the sin nature, others believe this is a _____ after salvation whereby God gives victory over sin so that a person can live within sin (but the sin nature is not eradicated).
2. What does the Bible teach concerning "_____"?
   a. The old nature was crucified in the _____ of Christ's death
   b. The old Adamic nature was *positionally* put to death with Christ. This does not mean the old nature is no longer active. Not at all. The old nature still has its _____.
   c. Eradication only happens at _____.
   d. The believer cannot put his sinful urges to death. He doesn't have the desire to crucify self, nor does he have the _____.
   e. The answer is to act on the _____ to crucify self.
   f. The Christian should: _____, not seek sin, _____, and claim the power over sin that comes from the accomplishments of the death and resurrection of Christ.

g. To take up one's cross is to _____ of Calvary to one's life.

The deeper life offered by Christ is the life of Christ living in and through the believer. It begins with the concept of _____. It happens at the conversion experience of every believer. To those believers who have to some degree understood and applied this doctrine to life, it has resulted in what they call "a deeper life." More correctly, union with Christ is the _____ of communion with Christ. When the believer attaches himself to Christ and depends on Christ in this earthly experience, he is walking in _____.

> Should the sense of remoteness persist in spite of prayer and what you believe is faith, look to your life for evidence of wrong attitudes, evil thoughts or dispositional flaws. These are unlike God and create a psychological gulf between you and him. Put away the evil from you, believe, and the sense of nearness will be restored. God was never away in the first place. – A. W. Tozer

Chapter Nineteen
The Experience of the Fullness of the Spirit

INTRODUCTION

1. This chapter explores the distinction between what might, for the lack of a better term, be called part of the "_____" Christian experience and those more _____ spiritual experiences more characteristic of revivalistic times.
2. Several biblical expressions are used by evangelicals to describe the relationship of the Holy Spirit to the believer:
    a. _____ of the Holy Spirit
    b. the Holy Spirit's _____
    c. the _____ of the Holy Spirit
3. Understanding the biblical uses of these terms provides a religious framework from which _____ with the Holy Spirit can be analyzed and understood.

THE BAPTISM OF THE HOLY SPIRIT

> ". . . you shall be baptized with the Holy Spirit not many days from now." – Acts 1:5

1. There can be a number of understandings and interpretations of the experiences recorded at Pentecost.

> "When the Day of Pentecost had fully come, they were all with one accord in one place. And suddenly there came a sound from heaven, as of a rushing mighty wind, and it filled the whole house where they were sitting. Then there appeared to them divided tongues, as of fire, and one sat upon each of them. And they were all filled with the Holy Spirit and began to speak with other tongues, as the Spirit gave them utterance." – Acts 2:1-4

2. It is clear from a reading of the passage that the Holy Spirit had a _____ in the activities and events recorded within the lives of the disciples.
3. A key to clearing up any confusion concerning Acts 2 is to recognize and understand the difference between the terms "_____" and "_____" as they relate to the work of the Holy Spirit.
    a. baptism of the Holy Spirit – *baptize* literally means, "to _____ or totally _____ something."
        1) Refers to a _____, in which the believer is placed into Jesus Christ
        2) Indicates the new believer's _____ in Christ
        3) "For by one Spirit we were all baptized into one body . . ." – I Corinthians 12:13

b. fullness of the Holy Spirit – *fullness* refers to placing something _____ and can carry with it the idea of _____.
   1) Christians are _____ by Paul to be filled with the Holy Spirit, as Ephesians 5:18 states, ". . . But be filled with the Spirit."
   2) fullness is a _____ experience
   3) indicates the believer is allowing the Holy Spirit to work through his/her life for _____

THE CHARACTERISTICS OF THE BAPTISM OF THE SPIRIT

1. _____
2. Non-repeatable (one time event)
3. _____ are placed in Jesus Christ
4. _____ in heaven
5. Occurs _____

Pentecostal Teaching Concerning the Baptism of the Holy Spirit:
1. Though some preach that the Baptism of the Holy Spirit is a _____ experience, where sin is eradicated from the believer's life, the example given in Scripture of the Corinthian church points otherwise.
   a. _____ at Corinth were said to be baptized into the Holy Spirit
   b. but, many of the Christians continued in _____
2. "The baptism of the Holy Spirit is an experience distinct from and usually subsequent to conversion in which a person receives the totality of the Spirit into his life and is thereby fully empowered for witness and service." – Anthony A. Hopkins (summary of Pentecostal theology)
3. According to the Assemblies of God denomination, "The Baptism of believers in the Holy Spirit is witnessed by the initial physical sign of speaking in other tongues. . . ." (*Statement of Fundamental Truths* – Article)

PENTECOSTAL VIEW OF THE BAPTISM OF THE SPIRIT

1. _____ (second work of grace)
2. Power for holiness and service
3. Comes by _____ and _____
4. Evidenced by _____
5. _____
6. Available to every Christian, but _____

Theology of the Baptism of the Holy Spirit:

WHEN DID THE BAPTISM OF THE HOLY SPIRIT OCCUR?	
THEOLOGICAL ANSWER:	In the death, burial and resurrection of Christ.
HISTORICAL ANSWER:	On the Day of Pentecost, the embryonic church was baptized with the Spirit.
EXPERIENTIAL ANSWER:	At the moment of my conversion, I was baptized into the body of Christ.
TESTIMONIAL ANSWER:	As I submitted to water baptism, I testified to my Spirit baptism.

1. Matthew 3:11 and Luke 3:16 both refer to the baptism of the Holy Spirit with fire. At least three interpretations have been offered to explain fire.

> "I indeed baptize you with water unto repentance, but He who is coming after me is mightier than I, whose sandals I am not worthy to carry. He will baptize you with the Holy Spirit and fire." – Matthew 3:11

   a. Little more than reference to the tongues of fire that appeared at _____ (Acts 2)

   b. _____

   c. The term "fire" is a _____ concerning the mission and ministry of the apostles.

THE INDWELLING OF THE HOLY SPIRIT

1. The significance of the indwelling of the Holy Spirit is seen when one considers the whole of Scripture. Consider the following regarding the fellowship that God seeks with His creation:

   a. in the _____, God walked and talked with Adam and Eve.

   b. after the _____, God spoke with men to have fellowship with them.

   c. God initiated a relationship with _____ and his descendents

   d. God instituted the development of a _____, which would contain "the dwelling place of God's glory"

   e. the glory of the Lord later dwelt in the _____

   f. "The Word became flesh and dwelt among us." – John 1:14

   g. today, God indwells _____ in the Person of the Holy Spirit

2. As a temple in which the Holy Spirit dwells – I Corinthians 6:19, even if a man had no concern about engaging in immoral activity, the thought of involving "the temple of God" in such a practice should help prevent him from sinning. When the Christian

realizes that he is never alone but that the Holy Spirit is always with him, ever present inside, he will be more cautious in his efforts to live for God.

3. The Bible teaches that the Spirit's indwelling occurs _____.
As Paul states, "Now if anyone does not have the Spirit of Christ, he is not His." – Romans 8:9

> **Characteristics of the Indwelling of the Spirit**
> 1. Enter all believers _____.
> 2. The basis of the _____.
> 3. _____.
> 4. _____, believer doesn't seek Him.
> 5. _____ results.

THE FULLNESS OF THE HOLY SPIRIT

> "And do not be drunk with wine, in which is dissipation; but be filled with the Spirit" – Ephesians 5:18

1. Unlike other ministries of the Spirit, the fullness of the Spirit is _____ and is the source of all spiritual experience in the life of the Christian.

2. "Let the preacher always confess before he preaches that he relies upon the Holy Spirit. Let him burn his manuscript and depend upon the Holy Spirit. If the Spirit does not come to help him, let him be still and let the people go home and pray that the Spirit will be him next Sunday." – Charles Haddon Spurgeon

3. "But one thing is needful. The Spirit did it all, on the day of Pentecost and afterwards. It was the Spirit who gave the boldness, the Spirit gave the wisdom, the Spirit gave the message, and the Spirit gave the converting power." – Andrew Murray

> **THE CHARACTERISTICS OF THE FILLING OF THE SPIRIT**
>
> 1. _____.
> 2. For living and service.
> 3. _____.
> 4. _____: "Not getting more of the Holy Spirit, but the Holy Spirit getting more of you."
> 5. _____.
> 6. _____ take advantage of it.

4. Various terms have been used to refer to the fullness of the Holy Spirit:
   a. "The _____ of the spirit." – John R. Rice

b. "It is His _____. Men are filled with the Spirit when they are prepared to abandon themselves to His dominion and to rejoice in his control." – Stuart Briscoe

c. "The _____ of the Spirit" – C. Sumner Wemp

5. A close reading of Ephesians 5:18 signifies the importance of being filled with the Holy Spirit:

a. God has given the Christian the _____ to be filled with the Spirit

b. the believer is _____ to be filled with the Spirit

c. the Greek indicates that the filling is a _____.

d. Summary: The Spirit's filling is a _____ thing. When a person is drunk, he is controlled by the substance within him; his _____ _____ are controlled. Similarly, when a believer is filled with the Holy Spirit, his _____ will be controlled by the Spirit.

6. This filling takes place as the believer experiences _____ with God through confession of sins (I John 1:9) and being yielded to Him. – Romans 6:13

7. Human _____ is involved in the filling of the Holy Spirit.

a. "If a man is clean and pure in heart and lives near God, he can always count on the operation of the Spirit of God . . . You can be filled with the light of the Spirit of life if you will obey the law." – F. B. Meyer

b. Romans 8:2 refers to "the law of the Spirit of life"

c. The human responsibility concerning the fullness of the Holy Spirit included both _____. As one yields his will to the Holy Spirit, he can by faith be filled with the Holy Spirit.

   1) "The Holy Spirit will fill us with His power the moment we are fully yielded." – Bill Bright

   2) Receiving the fullness of the Holy Spirit involves two expressions of faith: _____.

Though at times throughout Scripture, spectacular signs accompanied the fullness of the Holy Spirit. Does the Bible teach that these should be expected today? The Holy Spirit's fullness is primarily to produce the fruit of the Spirit – Galatians 5:22, 23. The outwards signs that were seen in the New Testament were given to verify the message being proclaimed. With the emergence of the revelation of God through His Word, the outwards signs are no longer necessary and consequently passed off the scene.

Chapter Twenty
The Experience of Seeking and Surrender

> "The meaning of being a Christian is that in response for the gift of a whole Christ I give my whole life to Him." – Alexander MacLaren

INTRODUCTION:

1. The experience of seeking God is not merely seeking an experience for _____ _____.
2. To seek God is to _____ after knowledge, love, fellowship.
3. Various abuses to the doctrine of "seeking" and "surrender" have existed throughout church history:
   a. _____.
   b. spending years in _____.
   c. praying with _____.
4. Various terms have been used to describe seeking and surrendering:
   a. the _____ life.
   b. the _____ life.
   c. the _____ life.
5. Consider the words of Charles Hadden Spurgeon, "If a Christian can by possibility be saved while he conforms to this world, at any rate it must be so as by fire. Such a bare salvation is almost as much to be dreaded as desired."
6. The idea of seeking and surrendering is fundamental to the Christian life, but the realization in a believer's life is more difficult than merely words can express.
   a. _____.
   b. _____.
   c. _____.
7. "The condition for obtaining God's blessing is *absolute surrender* to Him." – Andrew Murray

THE NATURE OF SURRENDER

> The terms *seeking* and *surrender* go hand in hand. When a Christian seeks God, it is a _____; when he surrenders, it is the end _____.

The Nature of Seeking and Surrender
1. Seeking is an _____ – it results in the believer surrendering himself to God.
2. A Christian does not _____ because he does not know how to surrender, or he may not have the strength to surrender.
3. It is necessary for the Christian to seek God to help him surrender certain aspects of his life that will keep him from experiencing the _____.

4. Throughout the _____ of seeking and surrender, there will be a natural progression in which seeking lead to surrender, which in turn leads to further seeking and further surrender, etc.

Scriptural Commands for Seeking and Surrender:

> "I beseech you therefore, brethren, by the mercies of God, that you present your bodies a living sacrifice, holy, acceptable to God, which is your reasonable service. And do not be conformed to this world, but be transformed by the renewing of your mind, that you may prove what is that good and acceptable and perfect will of God." – Romans 12:1, 2

1. The term "beseech" (Greek *parakalo*) is an appeal to a sentiment already existing in the heart.
2. "_____" is found in the aorist tense, indicating the idea that the believer should present himself or herself to God once and for all, not a _____. Consider the two aspects of surrendering to God.
   a. Initial surrender (once for all) – surrender to _____.
   b. Daily surrender for _____.

> "Surrender is not the surrender of the external life, but of the will; when that is done, all is done. There are very few crises in life; the great crisis is the surrender of the will. God never crushes a man's will into surrender, He never beseeches him, He waits until the man yields up his will to Him. That battle never needs to be re-fought." – Oswald Chambers

3. The term "body" is used to represent the _____.
   a. 'bodies' is the comprehensive term including the whole man, body, soul, and spirit – I Thessalonians 5:23. It is equivalent to 'yourselves.'
   b. "In fact the word body is a way of describing an organism _____." – Alva J. McClain
4. Perhaps the hardest aspect of surrender to God is found in the surrendering of the _____.
   a. It is evident from Scripture that though surrender is to be sought by the Christian; there is never in this life a time when the believer obtains a point where he no longer _____.
   b. Since there is no perfect _____ (sinless living), there is no perfect _____ (absolute surrender).
5. The idea of a *living sacrifice* carries with it several principles for the believer:
   a. It is a call to sacrifice that which is _____. – Genesis 22:2
   b. The laying on of hands on the sacrifice – Leviticus 1:4 carries with it an aspect of _____, for the individual is identifying with the sacrifice.
   c. _____ often accompanied the act of sacrificing, thus the believer identifies his sin with the sacrifice.

d. The _____ is burnt on the altar; ultimately resulting is a "sweet aroma to the Lord." – Leviticus 1:9, 13, 17

THE INTENSITY OF ABSOLUTE SURRENDER

1. Throughout Scripture numerous commands, promises, and illustrations instruct a Christian to _____.
2. To seek God means more than searching after a _____, because God is in all places present to reveal Himself to those who have eyes of faith to behold Him.
3. "Seeking God" is the sincere attempt to reestablish _____ _____ with God through intense prayer, concentrated Bible study, and unswerving obedience to the revelation of God.
4. The following charts will help to clarify the theology behind seeking God:

CONDITIONS FOR SEEKING GOD
_____ – Jeremiah 26:19
Brokenness – Jeremiah 50:4
Separation – Ezra 6:21
_____ – II Chronicles 7:14; 33:12
Desire – Psalm 119:10
_____ – Romans 9:32
_____ – Hebrews 11:6
Unity – Jeremiah 50:4
_____ – I Chronicles 16:10
Fear of the Lord – Hosea 3:5
_____ – Zephaniah 2:3

BARRIERS TO SEEKING GOD
Sin – Acts 17:30; Psalm 119:155
_____ – Psalm 10:4; Hosea 7:10
Ignorance – Romans 3:11; Acts 17:30
_____ – Isaiah 31:1
_____ – Romans 9:32
Failure to Confess Sin – Hosea 5:15
Wrong _____ – *see* Acts 8:18-24

SEEKERS AFTER GOD		
KINGS	1.	_____ – II Samuel 12:16
	2.	Asa – II Chronicles 14:7
	3.	Jehoshaphat – II Chronicles 17:4
	4.	_____ – II Chronicles 26:5
	5.	Jehoahaz – II Kings 13:4
	6.	_____ – II Chronicles 31:21
	7.	Josiah – II Chronicles 34:3
PROPHETS	1.	_____ – Deuteronomy 3:23
	2.	_____ – Daniel 9:3
	3.	Man of God – I Kings 13:6
APOSTLES	1.	_____ – II Corinthians 12:7, 8
MY PEOPLE CALLED BY MY NAME	1.	_____ – Exodus 33:7
	2.	Residue – Acts 15:7

The following chart gives some _____ examples of how those who loved God and wanted to please Him sought Him and acted out their faith. Today, the same principles have general applications for us, though we should not seek to slavishly follow every point.

STRATEGY FOR SEEKING GOD		
Preparation	Commitment to seek God expressed by:	
	1.	_____ – II Chronicles 15:12
	2.	Expression of desire – Psalms 119:10
	3.	Willingness to _____ – I Chronicles 16:10
	4.	_____ – II Chronicles 15:14
Process	1.	Study of Scripture – Psalms 119:94
	2.	_____ – Exodus 32:11; Ezra 8:32
	3.	Supplications – Daniel 9:3
	4.	_____ – II Samuel 12:16
	5.	_____ – Jeremiah 26:19
	6.	Obedience of Scripture – Ezra 7:10
Product	1.	Building of the _____ – I Chronicles 22:19
	2.	Keeping the _____ – II Chronicles 30:18, 19
	3.	_____ of the Law – Ezra 7:10

THE IMPLICATIONS OF SEEKING AND SURRENDER

1. The final result – _____ to the will of God – comes from _____ God.

2. The _____ is followed by a daily transformation and renewing of one's mind. – Romans 12:2

3. "As we study Chapter 6, 7, and 8 of Romans we shall discover that the conditions of living the normal Christian life are fourfold. They are (a) _____, (b) _____, (c) _____ ourselves to God, and (d) _____ in the Spirit . . . If we would live that life we shall have to take all four steps; not one or two or three, but all four. As we study each of them we shall trust the Lord by His Holy Spirit to illumine our understanding; and we shall seek His help now to take the first big step forward." – Watchman Nee

   a. _____ –

   > "Or do you not know that as many of us as were baptized into Christ Jesus were baptized into His death?" – Romans 6:3

      1) Often a Christian's actions result from _____, and they can only be changed when they are built on an accurate intellectual basis.
      2) When a Christian knows he was crucified with Christ, he should have _____. – Romans 6:3
      3) If we know the old man has received the _____ on the cross, we do not have to allow Satan to tempt and condemn us. – Romans 6:6
      4) When we know we are identified with Christ in the heavenlies, it becomes the basis for our _____.

   b. _____ –

   > "Likewise you also, reckon yourselves to be dead indeed to sin, but alive to God in Christ Jesus our Lord." – Romans 6:11

      1) Reckon carries with it the idea of "be counting on," or "_____."
      2) Part of the key to harmonizing our exalted _____ in heaven with our _____ on earth is to rely upon what we know to be true and to act accordingly – Romans 6:11

   c. _____ –

   > "And do not present your members as instruments of unrighteousness to sin, but present yourselves to God as being alive from the dead, and your members as instruments of righteousness to God." – Romans 6:13

      1) Based on what we know and how we have reckoned, we should _____ our lives on this earth to the designs of heaven. – Romans 6:13

2) Yieldedness involves giving God the "right of way" to every aspect of our lives. It is impossible for a Christian desiring to serve God consistently to divide the _____ in his life.

d. _____ –

"But God be thanked that though you were slaves of sin, yet you obeyed from the heart that form of doctrine to which you were delivered." – Romans 6:17

---

1) To obey Jesus is to recognize _____ in our lives.
2) The one who is the Lord of our lives is the one _____.
    – Romans 6:16, 17
3) When a Christian refuses to do the will of God, he is denying the lordship of Christ in _____.

"There must be a day in my life when I pass out of my own hands into His, and from that day forward I belong to Him and not to myself. . . . My giving of myself to the Lord must be an initial fundamental act. Then, day by day, I must go on giving to Him, not finding fault with His use of me, but accepting with praise even what the flesh finds hard. . . . Whatever He ordains for me is sure to be the very best, for nothing but good can come to those who are wholly His." – Watchman Nee

---

CHAPTER TWENTY-ONE
HABITS OF THE HEART,
HOW TO BUILD CHARACTER IN THE YOUNG

A. INTRODUCTION

(Taken from *Habits of the Heart*, a teaching video by Elmer Towns, Church Growth Institute, Lynchburg, VA, 1994)

1. Formation of Character

1. Thinking / Understanding

6. Habit / Accomplishments

2. Believe / Conviction

1. Character

5. Actions / Life

3. Expectations / Vision

4. Attitude / Values

2. Definition of character. Character is habitually doing the ___right thing___ in the ___right way___.

3. Character is result of your discipline. Where a ___spirituality___ results in inner power to do good, ___character___ results in your habits that make you do good. The believer needs both spirituality and character. One can have character without spirituality, but you can't have spirituality without habitually doing the right thing in the right way.

B. WHY WE MUST TEACH CHARACTER AND KNOW HOW IT IS FORMED

1. The public schools can no longer ___be trusted___ to do it.
2. Fewer ___models___ of character.
3. Influence of media and music.
4. Conflicting ___standards___ of secularization/humanization/etc.
5. Growing ___hostility___ of concept of Christian character and standards.
6. Growing ___lawlessness___, divorce, emotional problems, etc.
7. Teaching character is biblical, it ___obeys God___.

C. THINKING/KNOWING

When you change a person's _____, you influence their beliefs.

1. They must know they are _____. Morality begins when you recognize the child is "Beauty and the Beast." All have a dark side, yet great potential.
2. They must know there is a _____ between _____ _____ in the world, and that is reflected in their inner life.
3. They must know the gospel and _____.
4. They must know God's standards for _____.
5. They must know the _____ that God makes available for them to live above their natural circumstances.

D. BELIEF/CONVICTION

When you change a person's _____, you influence their expectations.

1. Belief is more than a decision to accept Christ. It is the _____ that something is true.
   a. I _____: I believe this plan will help me lose weight.
   b. I _____: I believe if I take pills, I'll lose weight.
   c. I am _____: I believe cutting calories will help me lose weight.
   d. I _____: I know fasting will help me lose weight.
2. Wrong expectations to change your life/character.
   a. You ask God to change a _____.
   b. You ask God to change your _____.
   c. You ask God to change _____.
3. _____ when you want to improve.
   a. You change your action without changing your thinking – _____
   b. You change once without permanent adjustments – _____
   c. You change outward without inward – _____
   d. You keep changing your thinking – _____
   e. You change your fruit without changing the root – _____
4. Your expectations must deal with _____
   a. There is a difference between "_____" and "I am a failure." Don't wear failure like a suit.
   b. Failure is _____. "Christ Jesus came into the world to save sinners, of whom I am chief." – I Tim. 1:15
   c. Don't let your failure _____. "Get Christians preoccupied with failure. From there on the battle is won" – C. S. Lewis, *Screwtape Letters*.
   d. _____ something from every failure.
   e. Take responsibility, _____.
5. _____, great character or great dreams? Does the person with character seek great dreams to live for God? Does the person with great dreams seek character to live for God?
   a. _____.

b. Those with great character but small dreams can be _____.

c. Those with great dreams but little character may be _____.

6. _____. Those with great dreams for God will develop character because they will be forced to live by standards outside themselves. They will not live a selfish life seeking only selfish pursuits.

E. ATTITUDE/VALUES

When you change a person's _____, you influence their actions.

1. An attitude is the _____ of your life's focus.

2. Who had the greatest influence on you growing up?
   Skill: _____
   Physical: _____
   Attitude: _____

3. What makes a person successful in work? Carnegie Institute found 15% _____ and 85% _____.

> Your personality is formed by attitudes and grows out of your character.

4. Why is a person fired? Incompetence _____, personality _____, other reasons _____.

5. You can't determine your circumstances, but when you have the right attitude you get the best out of circumstances and rise above your circumstances.

6. You can't determine your physical emotional response, but when you have the faith attitude, you can _____. You cannot _____ feelings, but you can keep your feelings from _____ you.

7. What do bad attitudes do to you?
   a. Sours our _____.
   b. Misdirects our _____.
   c. Dilutes our _____ and purpose.
   d. Jams our _____.
   e. Cuts us off from _____.

8. "If you think you are beaten, you are. If you think you dare not, you don't. If you'd like to win, but think you can't, it's almost certain you won't" – Old saying.

9. Excuses are really expressions of a bad attitude.
   a. Marriage fails because _____.
   b. Job stagnates because _____.
   c. School goes bad because _____.

10. Your lousy attitude is an _____, you can change it.

11. The pessimist _____ about the wind.

12. The optimist _____ a better wind.

13. The person with _____ changes the sail.

14. God chooses _____ we will go through; you choose _____ you will go through it.

> "Every time you make a choice, you are turning the control part of you into something a little different from what you were before. And taking your life as a whole, with all its innumerable choices, you are slowly turning the control thing either into a heavenly creature or into a hellish one." – C. S. Lewis

F. ACTIONS/LIFE

When you change a person's _____, you influence their habits.

1. The phrase "habits of the heart" was Tocqueville's description of America's virtue, character of morals.
2. Definition of habit: "A behavior pattern acquired by frequent repetition that is reflected in regular or increased performance."
3. Root: comes from root meaning "clothing that is usually worn," i.e., "_____ _____."
4. No one is without habits, _____ habits, and _____ habits.
5. Habits are _____ and _____.
6. Habits extend to every part of life.

	Language Habits	
Good		Bad
_____		_____
	Emotional Habits	
Good		Bad
_____		_____
	Physical Habits	
Good		Bad
_____		_____
	Instinctive Habits	
Good		Bad
_____		_____

7. "If you do _____, you'll be _____. – Erin Towns, Mother of Elmer Towns

G. CHARACTER BUILDING

When you change their _____, you influence their character.

1. A person with character is able to carry out a decision long after the emotion is gone that first motivated the choice.

2. Left side people   Right side people

   a. _____   a. _____
      based.   based.

   b. "What is   b. "What is
      _____?"   _____?"

   c. "When I feel good, then I'll   c. "When I do it, then I'll
      _____ it."   _____ good."

   d. Controlled by   d. Controlled by
      _____.   _____.

   e. _____   e. _____
      mindset.   mindset

   f. Life and lips   f. Life and lips
      _____   _____

   g. Looks for   g. Looks for
      _____   _____

   h. _____   h. _____
      influenced.   influenced.

   i. _____   i. _____
      during tough times   during tough times.

   j. This person   j. This person
      _____.   _____.

                                   – by John Maxwell

3. Right side people will have _____ friendships, _____ marriages, _____ vocations, and an _____ happiness.
4. How to step from the left side to the right side.

a. _____. Make a commitment to develop character. There is a life-changing energy in a volitional decision based on proper intellectual understanding; suggested by emotional commitment.

b. _____. Focus on right reasons for all you do. You must intentionally look beyond your emotions and social pressures to outward principles to guide your life.

> "But seek ye first the kingdom of God and His righteousness, and all these things shall be added to you." – Matt. 6:33, NKJV

c. _____. Establish a habit of doing things that are right. Doing the outward without inner understanding or commitment will not last nor will it form life's habits. But continual actions based on proper principles will mold character.

> "And whatever ye do, do it heartily, as to the Lord and not to men." – Col. 3:23, NKJV

d. Become _____ person focused. Don't live for your selfish happiness. True satisfaction is found on the road to service of other people.

> "For if you love those who love you, what reward have you? Do not even the tax collectors do the same?" – Matt. 5:46, NKJV

e. Be firm in your commitment, but be _____ and _____ with your inability to do all you desire.

> "Then said I: Lord God! Behold, I cannot speak, for I am youth. But the Lord said to me: Do not say, 'I am youth,' for you shall go to all to whom I send you, and whatever I command you, you shall speak." – Jeremiah's call, Jer. 1:6-7, NKJV

f. _____ your principles so that you remember your expectation and how to apply them.

> "Write the vision and make it plain on tablets, that he may run who reads it." – Hab. 2:2, NKJV

g. _____. When confronted with the problems and decisions of life, (a) look first to your principles, (b) gather all the facts you can, and (c) apply workable solutions.

"Brethren, I do not to count myself to have apprehended; but one thing I do forgetting those things which are behind and reaching forward to those things which are ahead, I press toward the goal of the prize of the upward call of God in Christ Jesus." – Phil. 3:13-14, NKJV